"I highly recommend this book for couples whose lives are being affected by sex addiction, not to mention clinicians working in the field. As with Paula Hall's other publications, it is clear, comprehensive, and keeps the needs of the reader in mind at all times. Not only does the book provide insight, it also offers a wealth of practical advice, getting down to the detail where it's most helpful. The author makes excellent use of real-life, client stories. This not only offers first-hand understanding of what it's like for couples to be caught up in sex addiction, but offers hope that things can and do get better. Paula Hall is a leading authority on sex addiction. This comes across in the book, making it an important and up-to-date addition to resources already available."

– **Dr Simon Draycott**, Chartered Counselling Psychologist, Chair of the ATSAC (Association for the Treatment of Sexual Addiction and Compulsivity)

"A book that offers hope to couples who otherwise wouldn't know where to turn or how to begin to heal from this destructive path. It will also be an invaluable guide to those who try to help them."

– **Philippa Perry**, psychotherapist, author, broadcaster

"At last, a well-written and accessible self-help guide to resolving one of the fastest-growing problems of our age – sex and pornography addiction. Every day I hear from couples whose relationship is being ruined by this blight – both those with the addiction and their part-ners are desperate for help. It's great there is now a reliable guide I can recommend."

– **Deidre Sanders** – Dear Deidre, agony aunt of The Sun

"Paula's book, part of a ground-breaking series looking at sexual addiction from multiple perspectives. This time the focus is on the couple relationship. Using her extensive knowledge and experience as a couple counsellor, linked with her expertise on sexual addiction, the book is sure to become a handbook for any counsellor working with couples in this area. It is full of relevant information, case work and most import-antly practical advice. This book differs from others in the series because it also focuses on how a counsellor can get the best use from the material with summaries at the end of a chapter to enable learning."

– **Peter Saddington**
Relate C

"I am so pleased that Paula Hall has taken on the difficult task of writing a book for couples in recovery from sex addiction! This has to be one of the most difficult topics to write about in a way that is honest, helpful, and hope-giving. Paula addresses the healing process with courage and in ways that encourage hope. Whether you are a clinician or a couple in recovery, you will find helpful and practical resources in this book around issues related to healing such as trauma, disclosure, trust-building, intimacy, and traumatic growth. While there is no 'one-size fits all' approach for any healing process, Paula has outlined many of the important guidelines and signposts for just such a journey."

> – **Barbara Steffens**, PhD, Licensed Professional Clinical Counselor (LPCC), Certified Clinical Partner Specialist (CCPS), and President of the Board of APSATS. Co-author of *Your Sexually Addicted Spouse: How partners can cope and heal* (Steffens & Means, 2009)

"This is a very welcome book, which provides practical and sensible help and advice for couples who face the relationship disruption resulting from a partner in the grips of a sexually addictive pattern of behaviour. Paula sensitively explores many of the taboos, stigmas and issues of isolating secrecy that these couples can experience in wider society. With great insight, she examines the difficulties people face in having this increasingly common and destructive problem recognised and treated. This is an excellent resource for couples and one that will be helpful to both experienced therapists and those in training."

> – **Andrew Yates**, Chair of COSRT (College of Sexual and Relationship Therapists)

"This groundbreaking book will lead couples in the direction of straight-forward actions toward healing individually and together – should they choose to do so. *Sex Addiction: A Guide for Couples and Those Who Help Them* fills a gap in helping couples use practical guidelines to re-launch their life together in the traumatic aftermath of infidelity, ultimately realizing the possibility of their intimate and sexual potential."

> – **Alexandra Katehakis**, PhD, author, *Sex Addiction As Affect Dysregulation: A Neurobiologically Informed Holistic Treatment*

"This is unquestionably the best guide I have seen for couples facing sex addiction. It provides the most up to date information and offers essential planning tools for moving forward into solid recovery. Paula Hall has an in depth understanding of the experience of sex addicts, their partners and the complexities of couple relationships. This book addresses all the myriad questions, doubts and fears of both partners and addicts as well as illustrating people's real life experiences in their own words. Couples will find that this book has the potential to change everything."

– **Linda Hatch**, PhD, CSAT, Author of
*Relationships in Recovery: A Guide for
Sex Addicts Who Are Starting Over*

Sex Addiction

Sex Addiction: A Guide for Couples and Those Who Help Them is a practical book that provides empathic support, guidance, information and pragmatic strategies for couples who want to survive sex and porn addiction – whether that's together, or apart.

Sex and porn addiction devastates couple relationships, and unlike the impact of infidelity, there is no 'before' to get back to and no 'after'. This book adopts the metaphor of a boat, presenting addiction as the tidal wave that devastates the relation-ship, leaving both crew members fighting for survival. There's guidance to ensure each partner makes it safely back to shore and advice on surveying the damage to your relation-ship and deciding if you want to save it and set sail again. You'll find practical advice for both the partner and the addicted partner, including first-hand accounts of couples that have already undertaken the journey. There are exercises to do alone, and many to share together, to help you understand what's happened, consider your future, and if you choose to stay together, begin the task of rebuilding trust and intimacy.

Sex Addiction is not only a practical guide for couples, but also for the therapists who support them. This book will be a companion to Paula Hall's previous books on sex addiction and builds on the already known frameworks and models used, but it is also written to stand alone.

Paula Hall is a UKCP-registered sexual and relationship psychotherapist, specialising in sex and porn addiction. She is Clinical Director of the Laurel Centre, which provides treatment services around the UK and accredited diploma-level training to professionals. She is also founder of the Hall Recovery Course and a founder trustee of ATSAC.

Sex Addiction

A Guide for Couples and
Those Who Help Them

Paula Hall

Routledge
Taylor & Francis Group

LONDON AND NEW YORK

First published 2019
by Routledge
2 Park Square, Milton Park, Abingdon, Oxon OX14 4RN

and by Routledge
52 Vanderbilt Avenue, New York, NY 10017

Routledge is an imprint of the Taylor & Francis Group, an informa business

© 2019 Paula Hall

British Library Cataloguing-in-Publication Data
A catalogue record for this book is available from the British Library

Library of Congress Cataloging-in-Publication Data
Names: Hall, Paula, author.
Title: Sex addiction : a guide for couples and those who help them / Paula Hall.
Description: Milton Park, Abingdon, Oxon ; New York, NY : Routledge, 2019. |
Includes bibliographical references and index.
Identifiers: LCCN 2018048235 | ISBN 9780815366102 (hardback : alk. paper) |
ISBN 9780815366119 (pbk. : alk. paper) | ISBN 9781351259996 (ebk)
Subjects: LCSH: Sex addiction. | Sex addiction–Treatment. |
Sex addicts–Family relationships.
Classification: LCC RC560.S43 H338 2019 | DDC 616.85/833–dc23
LC record available at https://lccn.loc.gov/2018048235

ISBN: 978-0-8153-6610-2 (hbk)
ISBN: 978-0-8153-6611-9 (pbk)
ISBN: 978-1-351-25999-6 (ebk)

Typeset in Times New Roman
by Newgen Publishing UK

MIX
Paper from
responsible sources
FSC C013056
www.fsc.org

Printed and bound in Great Britain by
TJ International Ltd, Padstow, Cornwall

Contents

Acknowledgements

My sincere thanks go to all the people who have helped me to write this much-needed guide for couples. Firstly, I want to thank the generous contributions from the couples that so kindly agreed to share their experiences of recovery throughout the pages of this book. Their contribution has been invaluable. I'd also like to thank my Clinical Associate Gabriel Dixon, who told me I 'had to write' this book – he was of course right, as he so often is! And my thanks also to my Senior Clinical Associate Nick Turner, who tirelessly read through each chapter and provided essential guidance and support. Thanks also to the whole team at the Laurel Centre, especially my Practice Manager Sonia Schillaci, for their patient support in my writing endeavours, and manning our ship during my seemingly endless absence. Last, and by no means least, I'd like to thank my clients, the many couples I have personally worked with, and those who have put their faith in the Laurel Centre, to help them recover from the devastating effects of sex and porn addiction. I'm pleased to say that most have saved their relationship, and many are enjoying a level of intimacy they'd never experienced before. And those who chose to end their relationship have done so in the confident knowledge that it was the right decision for them. Recovering from sex and porn addiction is a phenomenal challenge and I am privileged to have been part of that journey of recovery with couples, whether ultimately it resulted in re-launching their lives together, or apart.

Introduction

This has undoubtedly been the hardest book I have ever written, which is perhaps unsurprising as working with couples recovering from sex and porn addiction is, undoubtedly, the hardest work I've ever done. When I first trained with the UK couple counselling service Relate 25 years ago, we were warned that you can't work with 'split agendas', in other words, with couples who do not share the same vision for the future. That work is certainly difficult, but nowhere near as challenging as working with couples that have discovered they have little shared perception of the past, nor indeed of the present.

If helping couples recover from sex addiction is hard for the therapist that is of course nothing compared to the blood, sweat and tears facing those couples trying to decide if their relationship is worth saving, especially those who have children. Reconciling the chasm of difference that has suddenly erupted between them takes boundless courage and relentless empathy, for themselves as well as for each other. And first and foremost, it requires understanding why and how they have become so estranged from each other, on opposite sides of the addiction abyss that divides them.

The person with the addiction and their partner are in completely different places. Most commonly, the addicted partner is desperate to save the relationship, a relationship that their actions alone have devastated, along with the person in their life they claim to love the most. Partners are frequently too traumatised and disorientated to know what they want; on the one hand, they want the old familiarity and security of the relationship, while simultaneously questioning if anything they experienced in the past was ever real.

For the addicted partner, getting into recovery is a gift, a new start, an opportunity to truly embrace and celebrate life. For the partners, discovering sex or porn addiction is like stepping on a landmine, it's the day their 'normal' life was brutally snatched away. One half of the couple is celebrating a baptism, while the other is mourning at a funeral. For the addicted partner it is the end of a waking nightmare; for the partner, it's the start. As one addicted partner profoundly shared, "*I gained my freedom at the cost of hers*".

Fortunately, the devastation is not so dramatic for all couples, but nonetheless, discovering addiction heralds a turning point in both partners' lives and in their relationship, and all couples must decide which way to turn. The journey is often a long one and a lonely one, and it is my sincere hope that this book will be a guide to help you consider which way to go. Throughout this book you will read the experiences of the generous couples that have kindly shared their story, couples that have already undertaken the journey and want you to be encouraged and supported in the decisions that you make, and perhaps learn from some of the mistakes they made along the way.

Those who have read my other books, or have worked or trained with me, will know how much I love using metaphors to explain complex processes and make them memorable. This guide for couples will use the metaphor of a boat in a storm. The boat represents the relationship and the discovery of sex or porn addiction is the tidal wave that capsizes the boat. The couples are crew members, each responsible for their individual survival and the decision whether to rescue the relation-ship or not. Those who choose to stay together will need to develop the tools to rebuild their boat, or perhaps fashion a new one, better equipped for the journey ahead. Those who separate need to ensure they don't go down with the ship and steer towards other shores, mindful of any other crew members on board, such as children. I hope this metaphor will help you to reflect individually and jointly on the quality of your relation-ship, your roles as partners and the direction you wish your lives to go.

Part I focuses on surviving the impact of the tidal wave of sex or porn addiction, providing information and tools to help each of you get safely back to shore, without unconsciously sabotaging whatever may be left of your relation-ship. Part II is all about developing understanding about what has happened, what it means to you as individuals and what it means for your relationship. You'll find chapters on the importance of full disclosure and exercises to help improve communication and learn more about each other's reality. You'll also find a chapter devoted to the decision about whether you want to salvage your relationship. Part III is about how you'll move on if you separate, with practical advice on how to ensure you separate in a healthy way as well as guidance on how to minimise any harmful effects on children. Part IV is about moving on together and includes chapters on rebuilding trust, forgiveness and developing and deepening intimacy.

This book cannot tell you if your relationship will survive, but I hope it will make the journey of discovery smoother. There may be some parts of this book that will be painful to read, hard truths that the addicted partner has to accept as a consequence of their addiction and challenging realities for partners who choose to stay with them. I have endeavoured to write this from both perspectives, so each of you will benefit; I have tried to be fair, even-handed and sensitive to both partners' needs, but regrettably addiction is not fair, and whether together or apart, both of you have to live with the consequences.

Part I

Surviving the storm

Part I includes four chapters that focus on surviving the impact of the tidal wave on your relation-ship, both as individuals and as a couple. Chapter 1 will explain why sex addiction devastates couple relationships and how it differs from the impact of infidelity and other addictions. Chapter 2 expands to allow readers to understand more about what sex addiction is and what it means to struggle with sex or porn addiction, or find out that you're living with someone who does. The importance of individual recovery is covered in Chapter 3, as readers are encouraged to ensure they are each safely back on shore before deciding what to do with their relationship. In Chapter 4 you'll find lots of practical strategies and advice, including communication techniques, accountability and check-in sessions to help couples survive the tumultuous impact of the tidal wave and ensure they don't inadvertently cause themselves or each other any further harm.

Chapter 1

Why sex and porn addiction hurts so much

The tidal wave

Having worked as a couple counsellor for 25 years, I can honestly say that nothing impacts a couple relationship in such a devastating way as sex addiction. For the addicted partner, this is a catastrophe they've been trying to avoid for years. They know their relation-ship has been sailing too close to the wind for a long time, but they have done everything in their power to remain captain of the boat and avoid disaster. For partners, they may have assumed their relation-ship was cruising along on calm waters, give or take a few turbulent times, completely unaware of the storm brewing on the horizon. Perhaps they'd noticed dark clouds looming and building, but had no idea where they were from or what they meant. Discovering sex or porn addiction, however that happens, is a tidal wave that devastates the relation-ship and leaves both crew members fighting for survival. The person with the addiction may be left desperately trying to bail out water, doing anything they can to stop the ship from sinking, while the partner is thrown overboard, simply trying not to drown.

So why is sex and porn addiction so devastating? For the partner it combines the most destructive ingredients of personal pain – betrayal, sexual infidelity, deceit and shame. It combines both the well-known devastation of an affair with the torment and challenges of addiction. For the person with the addiction, it's their worst nightmare. They grapple with a crippling fear of losing the person they purport to love most in the world and everything else they've ever held dear: their children, their family, their friends, possibly their career and reputation. And on top of that, they carry the shame of having their greatest secret discovered and losing an aspect of themselves they've secretly relied on to maintain their emotional stability. Both feel exposed, vulnerable and bewildered and almost certainly further apart from each other than they ever could have imagined.

There are three main reasons why sex and porn addiction hurts couple relationships so much. Firstly, it wrecks trust; secondly, it damages intimacy; and finally, the social stigma and ignorance that surrounds the problem isolates them from the rest of the world.

How addiction wrecks trust

Healthy relationships are built on trust. Trusting that the other keeps their commitments, large and small. That they'll always have your best interests at heart and will stand by you in good times and bad.

The impact on a partner's trust is perhaps easier to understand. They discover that the person they've committed to has been leading a double life. They have lied, deceived, cheated and manipulated the other into believing either that their relationship was safe and sound, or that any problems they faced were caused by something else, perhaps even the partner themselves. Of course, not all relationship difficulties will be caused by the undisclosed addiction, but the addiction will almost certainly have exacerbated them and prevented them from being addressed appropriately.

Partners find themselves not only unable to trust their addicted partner, but also feeling unable to trust their own ability to make accurate judgements of the people and the world around them. We all assume we're a good judge of character, and in particular, we assume we know the person we have chosen to spend our life with. But when you discover addiction, everything you thought you knew and all the assumptions you had made are shattered in a second. Partners describe how they find themselves becoming suspicious of everyone – after all, if the person you're closest too has successfully held such a big secret as this, perhaps there are others. And they doubt their ability to know if their thoughts, feelings and instincts are correct. If they were wrong about their addicted partner, perhaps they're also wrong about many other things, such as their choice of friends, career or hobbies. Partners describe themselves as being in free-fall with nothing solid and secure to hold on to.

But sex and porn addiction damages the addicted partner's trust too. They may have spent years living in doubt about the love within their relationship. Doubting their own feelings towards their partner and questioning 'how could I do this if I truly loved them?' They also doubt their partner's love for them, knowing that their partner is loving only part of the reality of who they are and would probably have never chosen to be with them if they had known the whole truth, or where their relationship might end. People with addiction often struggle with what's known as imposter syndrome, a sense of being a fraud who doesn't really belong in the relationship or in the family. And that sense of not belonging often extends to their friendships and working life, leaving them with a constant sense that if people really knew who they were, they wouldn't be acceptable or allowed to be part of the group. Addiction robs people of their trust in their own identity as well as their ability to trust that others really love them, or indeed care about them.

How the discovery or disclosure process impacts trust

The disclosure or discovery process for most couples is rarely straightforward and, ultimately, is always chaotic. In *Sex Addiction – The Partner's Perspective* I describe the four most common ways the truth is finally revealed – we'll review each of those briefly here and how they impact trust.

The sledgehammer blow – this describes how it feels when everything comes out all at once. For some, it's the discovery of physical evidence, such as an online profile or videos; for others, it's the discovery of an STI or being sacked from work; for some couples, it's a revelation from a third party, such as someone they've acted out with or, for a few, the police. These sledgehammer blows come without warning and as the tidal wave hits, the first emotion experienced by both is usually shock. There is no time for either partner to prepare themselves psychologically or emotionally and both are likely to feel traumatised. Trust is instantly lost.

The drip, drip disclosure – this is probably the most common disclosure process as the addicted partner slowly reveals their activities over an extended period of time. The process may have started with a discovery of some kind and then in an attempt to minimise the pain caused to a partner, the addicted partner waits for each new reality to be absorbed before revealing another. They're terrified of their relation-ship capsizing, thinking a series of small tidal waves will be less painful than one big one. Meanwhile, the partners find themselves with a growing sense of anxiety and dread, having no idea when the next wave will come. Trust has been obliterated, piece by piece, but partners daren't even trust themselves to start coming to terms with the pain, lest that simply makes pain for more.

The drip, drip, drip exposure – like the drip, drip disclosure, this is a process that can be dragged out for many weeks or months. But the discoveries are due to the partner's unwavering efforts to reveal the truth, rather than the addicted partner's confessions. Using our tidal wave metaphor, the addicted partner will have been furiously denying there was any storm ahead and no more water would get into their boat, but the partner sensed the storm in the air, and ultimately was proved right. These couple relationships tend to be the most fraught with anger and resentments as suspicions continue long after the full story is revealed.

The detective breakthrough – when addictive behaviours are discovered by partners all at once, there will probably have been tell-tale signs in the relationship for some time. These couples have often had a challenging relationship, either fraught with conflict or a frustrating sexual relationship. The addicted partner will have continued to hide their addiction, but the partner, knowing something is wrong, finally makes a dramatic breakthrough. These couples are most likely to feel a sense of shared relief that the truth is finally out, but that is accompanied by shock and fear that what they had once shared had never been real in the first place.

The impact on intimacy

Intimacy is a very difficult concept to define. We talk a lot more about the different elements of intimacy and how to rebuild it in Chapter 14, but here we're going to focus on how sex and porn addiction damages intimacy within a couple relationship, not just when it's discovered, but over the years of active addiction that precede disclosure.

Trust is the bedrock of intimacy – when it's there, we assume we're safe to be open and vulnerable with each other. To share our innermost doubts and fears, hopes and joys. But when trust is gone, intimacy soon follows. But for couples whose relationship has been overshadowed, knowingly or unknowingly, by sex or porn addiction, intimacy, at least in some areas of the relationship, will be limited. However, that doesn't mean that there will have been no intimacy in the relationship at all. Some books written about sex addiction, especially those written pre-Internet porn, will tell you that addiction is an intimacy disorder and sex addicts can't do intimacy. These kinds of blanket statements are damaging to couples as it can leave both of them fearing the whole of their relationship was meaningless and a charade. And couples who had previously experienced themselves as loved and cherished by each other can find themselves questioning their ability to know how real love feels. It's true that before the days of Internet porn a high percentage of people with sex addiction were people who had come from backgrounds with inadequate or abusive parenting, and the result of their childhood experiences left them finding it difficult to have meaningful and intimate relationships in adult life. However, the profile of someone with sex or porn addiction has changed considerably over the years and there are now many, many people who are able to have full, intimate and loving relationships – and act out.

However, the secrecy and shame of sex and porn addiction inevitably erode intimacy for most couples. As the addictive behaviour escalates, either by spending more and more time online viewing porn or going offline into live sexual encounters, there is less and less energy for the relationship. The person with the addiction often withdraws from emotional communication as their guilt and shame grows. Partners usually sense this withdrawal, and without an explanation may find themselves either getting into more and more conflict over the lack of intimacy or withdrawing from the relationship themselves for protection.

Another intimacy area that is affected by sex and porn addiction is a couple's sex life. Some people with sex addiction completely withdraw from any kind of sexual relationship, while some never engaged from the start. Others withdraw more gradually, either by wanting less and less sexual contact or being unable to be fully present during sex. Many addicted partners describe how high levels of porn use have changed their sexual tastes and subsequently they feel less and less sexually fulfilled with their partners. Partners report feeling pressured to go beyond their sexual comfort zones or noticing that the addicted partner always seemed distracted during sex, while others feel sexually rejected and can struggle with sexual frustration and low sexual self-esteem as their addicted partner seems to inexplicably lose interest in them.

It's also now widely recognised that compulsive pornography use can lead to sexual dysfunctions (Park et al., 2016). In the first instance there may be difficulty reaching orgasm, then problems getting aroused and getting an erection. This is often referred to as PIED – Porn-Induced Erectile Dysfunction. As these dysfunctions become an increasing element of a couple's sexual interaction, both may withdraw further from sexual intimacy to avoid what may feel like sexual failure. And for many, one strategy to avoid sexual intimacy is to withdraw from any kind of physical intimacy and hence affection also erodes. Regrettably, as the couple's sexual relationship diminishes, porn use may escalate as an alternative and hence a negative cycle of intimacy withdrawal and porn viewing ensues. And as is the case for many couples, as the sexual connection is lost, they become less intimate and feel more distant in other areas of their relationship.

However, this is not always the case. For some couples, the kind of sexual intimacy they shared has not changed over the years. Many people with sex addiction will always have enjoyed the intimacy of sex in their primary relationship, but split off their need for other types of sexual experience into acting out. However, discovering sex or porn addiction always changes sexual intimacy. For a few, the fear of loss may temporarily fuel their libido, a common experience after infidelity, but as the shock wears off, most will need to reclaim and rebuild their sexual relationship.

How social stigma and ignorance isolates couples

Once the tidal wave hits, and the cause is identified as sex or porn addiction, couples are often left isolated and alone as individuals and also isolated and alone as a couple. Sex and porn addiction is still widely misunderstood and shrouded in secrecy and shame, leaving couples unsure where to turn for help and support. Regrettably, there also continues to be a woeful lack of professional help, meaning couples who turn to relationship counsellors untrained in the area of addiction can inadvertently do more harm than good. And those who go for professional help as individuals may find they are receiving different information and advice which can inevitably lead to further conflict within the couple relationship.

Sex and porn addiction are not like any other addictions because they damage the very core of our humanity – our relationships. Sexual identities are left in shatters with partners often feeling they have been sexually abused by the deceit and betrayal and addicted partners feeling like the perpetrator of that abuse. As discussed in length in both accompanying books, the label of co-dependency is at best unhelpful, at worst inaccurate and damming. Any recovery programme that fails to have healthy sexuality at the centre can leave the addicted partner feeling castrated.

There are a number of myths around sex and porn addiction that hurt couples, which we will now explore.

It's all about infidelity

There's no doubt that partners of sex addicts feel a profound sense of betrayal that is similar to the feelings experienced by people who have been betrayed by an affair, including partners of porn addicts where there has been no physical infidelity. Similarly, people struggling with addiction have been adulterers, they have committed a similar act, whether that betrayal has been paid for, with a stranger, with someone known or with people or images online, but there are essential differences that make this comparison unhelpful.

Firstly, affairs are nearly always a symptom of a problem within the relationship or are a consequence of a significant relationship breakdown. The boat is broken, that's why it crashed. When the problem of addiction is approached like an infidelity, then each member of the couple may look to their relationship as the cause, rather than recognising it is the addicted partner who is responsible. The comparison to affairs can also leave couples fearing they're over-reacting and not trusting the emotional impact, especially when well-meaning friends make references to others they know who've had an affair or storylines in the media or on screen.

Another key difference to infidelity is that there is no 'before' and there may be no 'after'. In almost every case, the sexually compulsive behaviour pre-dates the relationship, and someone with an addiction will always be in recovery. Generally speaking, couples 'get over' an affair, or separate. Couples recovering from sex and porn addiction have quite a different battle, as this book will continue to explore.

Having said all that, there are of course some people with sex addiction who 'also' have an affair. Part of their acting out behaviour may involve developing romantic attachments as well as sexual ones, sometimes referred to as love addiction, or they may have developed a longer-term relationship with one of their casual acting out partners. When this happens, the infidelity is a consequence of the addiction. The secrecy and the double life of compulsive behaviours alongside the gradual erosion of intimacy within the couple relationship create the environment where an affair is more likely to take place.

Sex addicts are perverts

This is perhaps the opposite end of the spectrum to 'it's like infidelity', in the sense that rather than normalising it as something that many people have struggled with, it's a problem that is extreme and dangerous.

While all addictions struggle with a social stigma, be that alcohol, drugs or gambling, none are as bad as sex addiction. When I'm delivering training to professionals I always start with a word association game to help them consider how sex addiction is viewed. Common words include sad, selfish, a player, greedy, pervert, desperate, lonely, weird, out-of-control, loser, grandiose, greedy, needy. These negative and character-damning labels affect not only the person with the addiction but also the partner. Regrettably, there is still a perception by much of the public and some uneducated professionals that sex or porn addiction is in some way akin to sexual offending. That anyone whose sexual behaviours have become out of control is in some way a risk to others. Unfortunately, there are some people with porn addiction who have escalated to viewing images under the age of 18 and may find themselves facing prosecution, but this is a consequence of the addiction, rather than an event that describes their sexual template. Similarly, someone who finds their sexual tastes have become more extreme, a common consequence of porn (Wéry & Billieux, 2016), will wonder if this is the root of their problem and their partner questions if they can ever be enough, but this is a consequence.

The myth that all sex addicts are perverts adds an additional layer of fear, shame and stigma onto couples who need help. It can leave them questioning themselves and each other, rather than getting into recovery and focusing on whether their relationship has a future.

When there has been offending behaviour

Couples who are struggling to overcome sex or porn addiction where there has also been offending, such as viewing sexual images under the age of 18 or being caught engaging in exhibitionist or voyeuristic behaviours, are likely to find themselves feeling even more isolated and stigmatised than others. It's essential to find services that can support both of you, independently and together, as you work through the impact on your relationship as well as the legal ramifications.

Once an addict, always an addict

For most people, recovering from addiction is a lifetime commitment – but that doesn't mean it's a constant challenge or a painful process. And it most certainly doesn't mean that the person with the addiction hasn't changed. On the contrary, many people who are in recovery would say that they have made profound personal changes that have significantly improved every area of their life.

How an addicted partner feels about being in recovery will have an impact on the partner. And similarly, how a partner feels about living with someone in recovery will impact the addict partner (you'll find much more on this in Chapter 11). You can either see recovery as a burden or as a gift. You can focus on the restrictions it puts on your life, or you can see all the new doors that are opening up. I know it's a cliché, but discovering and acknowledging addiction is a learning opportunity. And if you do decide to give your addicted partner a second, or even third or fourth chance, then the consequence may be that you are both able to appreciate more and work harder than those who have never faced such challenges.

Addiction is just an excuse

Even if this isn't actually said it is often implied in the comments and questions raised by friends and professionals alike when partners talk about the discovery or disclosure of sex addiction. This statement usually says much more about the speaker than it does about the partner and demonstrates their shock and disbelief. A more helpful and more accurate statement would be "It's hard to comprehend that someone can act out in the ways they have and keep it so completely hidden". But in reality, that is precisely what happens in sex addiction.

The assumption that a partner 'must' have had some inkling is supported further when hindsight is confused with unconscious knowing, or what some addiction professionals might even call denial. For example, when a partner reflects on their past and says "He did seem to spend a huge amount of time on his computer" or "he said he couldn't be contacted abroad because his phone didn't work there" and they now realise they must have been acting out, that is most likely hindsight. Hindsight develops when we look back at an event of the past with new knowledge from today and create a different, often more accurate picture. We all have times when we have experienced hindsight, be that an adolescent's secret party, a friend's relationship breakdown or a workplace making redundancies. The fact that you can see clearly now does not mean that you were in denial or should have known earlier.

When professionals, therapists or friends interpret hindsight as unconscious knowing it can add further shame and self-doubt to partners. It is natural for partners to wonder if they should or could have seen the signs, but often there are none. What's more, partners are usually busy getting on with their own lives and have no reason to assume their addicted partner is doing anything untoward.

Unlike other addictions, sex addiction is invisible and can exist and flourish while remaining completely and totally concealed.

He/she is not who you thought they were?

In many ways, this is the opposite of the above and is frequently offered as words of encouragement and support. The intention of the statement is often to reduce a partner's shame by saying 'you wouldn't be with them if you'd known who they were'. And while it may be true in part, statements like this can increase feelings of shame and self-doubt because it says that you made a mistake about the whole person, rather than not knowing about the addiction. So everything about the addict is brought into question – their personality and character, their relationships with others, their history, their likes and dislikes.

Thinking that you did not know your addicted partner can leave partners feeling bereft of everything they've known and enjoyed in the past. Flooded with endless questions, partners may wonder if they were really loved at all. Was everything a sham and a lie?

It seems to be much easier to recognise chemical addictions as an illness or a condition that someone has rather than a problem that someone is. If someone develops alcoholism, their life before the addiction is not brought into question. But when someone has sex addiction, their whole being is now open to debate. In reality, sex and porn addiction are like the other addictions in so much as it's a problem that someone has, not who someone is. What partners didn't know was that they were living with someone who has sex addiction, but that doesn't mean that everything else they knew about them was untrue. It is perfectly possible (and very common) for someone with sex or porn addiction to be a loving partner, a devoted mother or father, a pillar of the community, a trustworthy, kind, sensitive and moral person. Everything you thought they were was true, but there is now an additional piece that you didn't know about. A piece you may not want to live with.

You're over-reacting

Thankfully, there are very few friends or professionals who would say this out right, but sometimes misguided attempts to make the problem feel more manageable have the same effect.

Most commonly, a well-meaning friend may minimise what's happened by making broad generalisations based on their experiences and their perception of societal norms. Interestingly, what's perceived as 'normal' varies widely depending on the gender and orientation of the partner and the person with the addiction. So typically a male addict's behaviour may be minimised as 'just what men do'. Or if you're in a gay relationship your assumption or definition of fidelity may be challenged as 'not realistic'. Partners of female sex addicts find their problem minimised in a different way, as friends may suggest that they're 'lucky to be with such a sexual woman'. Indeed, male partners often have the hardest time getting understanding from their male friends.

Another way in which partners' pain is minimised is when the media and so-called professionals dismiss that sex and porn addiction exist. Or they misdiagnose or mislabel yet another wayward celebrity to excuse their indiscretion. It is profoundly hurtful for partners to read that sex or porn addiction is not real when they are the innocent victims of the painful truth and reality.

Sex addiction is unlike any other addiction because it violates the very core of a couple's intimate relationship, and at the time of writing this book, it is still something that is commonly misunderstood within our culture. So not only do partners have to experience the personal pain and betrayal of sex addiction, they often also feel betrayed by professionals and society.

Finally, a healthy couple relationship is based on equality; on sharing a common narrative, of the past, present and future; on knowing each other. When compulsive behaviours are hidden, the secret means that one person is unknown. Back to the boat metaphor. The addicted partner knew there was something stowed in the hold of their relation-ship – the partner didn't even know there was a hold. During their life together, the addicted partner has frequently absconded from the boat and visited other shores, the partner thought they were on the same journey together. In reality, neither was truly sharing the same relation-ship.

References

Park, B.Y., Wilson, G., Berger, J., Christman, M., Reina, B., Bishop, F., Klam, W.P., Doan, A.P. (2016) Is internet pornography causing sexual dysfunctions? A review with clinical reports. *Behavioural Sciences*, 6(3): 17.

Wéry, A., Billieux, J. (2016) Online sexual activities: An exploratory study of problematic and non-problematic usage patterns in a sample of men. *Computers in Human Behaviour*, 56: 257–266.

Chapter 2

Understanding the reality of sex addiction

The tidal wave – 101

In this chapter we're going to explore what sex addiction is, what lies at the root of it and why people find it so difficult to stop, even when they want to. You'll also find some questions to help you to confirm if sex addiction is what your relationship is facing. You'll find a lot more information on understanding sex and porn addiction, as well as specific chapters for female sex addiction, people of faith, and those from GSRD (gender, sexual and relationship diverse) communities, and those who have crossed the line into offending behaviours in my other book, *Understanding and Treating Sex and Pornography Addiction* (2018, Routledge).

What is sex addiction?

The term sex addiction describes any pattern of out-of-control sexual behaviour that causes problems in someone's life. Porn addiction is a subset of sex addiction and describes behaviours that are purely related to the viewing of sexual images, usually on the Internet. There are many different types of sexual behaviour that can become addictive and it's not the type of behaviour that defines it as an addiction, but the dependency on it, in the same way as the type of alcohol does not define alcohol addiction, but the dependency on how alcohol makes you feel and, crucially, the inability to stop in spite of negative consequences.

To understand any kind of addiction, it's important to know that it's much, much more than simply a bad habit. Addictions are both biological and psychological; they are strategies used to alleviate negative emotions and create positive ones, strategies that change the way the brain is wired up to the point that it's difficult to function normally without them. What starts as a way of managing difficult emotions gradually becomes a way of coping with life.

The biology of addiction

Pleasure is a physical process triggered by chemicals in the brain – primarily dopamine, endorphins and adrenalin. These chemicals are all naturally occurring and someone with a chemical addiction heightens the impact of these chemicals by introducing others, whereas someone with a behavioural addiction, such as gambling, sex or porn, uses their behaviour to develop a super-fast highway in their brain to reach them faster. Primarily, addiction is fuelled by the chemical dopamine. A chemical that makes us want and seek out reward, but not a chemical that alone gives us pleasure. Hence some people with addiction find themselves getting hooked on activities that they don't even enjoy.

The brain is made up of millions of neural pathways that carry the necessary messages that make us think, feel and act and there is a specific set of pathways responsible for delivering the feelings of pleasure. If we always access those pathways in the same way, they will become stronger and other pathways that might have previously been used to access the pleasure chemicals become weaker. This is the principle of learning – the more we do something, the better we get at it. But in addiction, while those pathways become more fixed they also become less effective at delivering the desired effect, which is why addicts find they need more stimulation in order to get the same affect (Blum et al., 2000; Kuhn & Gallinat, 2014). This is what's known within the addiction field as tolerance and escalation.

As well as changes in the reward pathways, people with addiction often experience difficulties with impulse control, deferring gratification and making judgements about harmful consequences – all processes that involve the frontal cortex of the brain and underlying white matter (Messina et al., 2017). These areas of the brain are altered by addiction and as they are still maturing in adolescence, this is why early exposure is believed to be a significant factor in the development of addiction.

Internet pornography can be especially easy to get hooked on because of the way it works on the brain, because it is a 'supernormal stimuli'. A supernormal stimuli is the term used when we find our biological drives and instincts override our common sense, such as when we gorge ourselves on beautiful cupcakes or, for the addict, lose hours looking at porn. Our brains naturally seek novelty and the drive for both food and sex are essential survival strategies. Internet pornography provides endless opportunities for novelty and reward and it's suggested that it's the perfect laboratory for witnessing neuroplastic changes (Hilton, 2013).

Addiction is a disease of the brain that disrupts the circuitry of the brain and challenges control. Continued chemical misuse or behavioural acting out changes the chemistry of the brain and the brain literally becomes dependent on the chosen drug or activity to feel pleasure and reduce pain. But brains can change back. They can be re-wired.

The psychology of addiction

Some people refer to addictions as anaesthetising behaviours; ways of numbing out the stresses and pains of everyday life. Others refer to addictions as hedonistic behaviour; a way of seeking perpetual pleasure. Often it's both, or at least that's how it starts, but over time the drug of choice, be that sex, cocaine, alcohol or food, creates the very problems the addict is trying to numb out and provides very limited pleasure indeed.

In some respects you could argue that all of human behaviour is based on our desire to increase or elicit a positive feeling state and reduce or eliminate a negative one. We are pre-programmed to seek pleasure and avoid pain as a survival mechanism. Surely that's why there are magazines in doctor's waiting rooms? Rather than focus on our illness, anxiety or boredom, we can distract ourselves with something more interesting. We all have a multitude of techniques and methods for cheering ourselves up and calming ourselves down. Hopefully, most of them are healthy. People with addictions are no different except that their drug of choice has often become their only, and increasingly ineffective, coping mechanism. For someone with sex or porn addiction, rather than finding appropriate and healthy ways of regulating emotion, watching porn, fantasising about sex, or having sex has become their primary coping mechanism. It is the only method they have for managing life; a life that is often becoming increasingly painful and unmanageable.

Sex and porn addiction are particularly powerful mood-altering drugs because there is such a wide assortment of sexual experiences or porn genres that can elicit a range of emotional responses. In the same way as some drug users will mix and choose between uppers, downers and hallucinogenics, the sex or porn user can choose behaviours that will give a range of feeling states. In short, sex and porn addiction are maladaptive coping strategies that are driven by psychological pain, not sexual desire.

Sex addiction and sex drive

One of the most common misconceptions about sex and porn addiction is that it's linked to sexual desire. In my clinical experience, backed up by a growing body of research, neither sex nor porn addiction is the same as a high sex drive (Stulhofer, 2016). Many of the men and women with addiction I've worked with do not get sexual pleasure from what they're doing and it does not satiate their drive. In fact, some would go so far as to say they consider themselves to have a very low sex drive or indeed that their addiction has robbed them of their libido.

While their compulsive behaviours are sexual in some respect, the primary motivation is not satiation of sex drive, a fact that is essential for couples to understand. Sex and porn addiction are not driven by the physical essence of libido but by the psychological need to satisfy a deeper emotional need, or to satisfy biological craving in the brain. If you consider a typical porn addict who might spend up to seven or eight hours online at a time, postponing ejaculation for as long as possible, it doesn't make sense that the goal is to satiate sexual drive. The real motive for such behaviour is escaping from reality and enjoying the aroused brain state, even more than genital stimulation.

In many ways, sex addiction has more in common with eating disorders than it does with other addictions (Goodman, 1993). In one study by Patrick Carnes (1991), 38 per cent of his sample had an eating disorder, and in the UK 79 per cent of those with another addiction cited eating disorder (Hall, 2018). In the same way that bulimia, anorexia and compulsive over-eating are about an unhealthy relationship with food, sex addiction is an unhealthy relationship with sex. In healthy individuals, both sex and food satisfy a natural, innate and primitive drive, but when the relationship becomes distorted, sex addiction has no more to do with sex drive than eating disorders do with hunger.

However, there are definitely some who suffer with sex or porn addiction who think that they do have a high sex drive and describe their initial motivation for acting out as being a way of meeting their sexual needs, but further investigation and exploration of their feelings often expose this as mistaken. In the same way as someone with an eating disorder might misinterpret feelings of hunger or fullness, so someone with sex addiction can misinterpret their sexual desire. When sex, porn or food are used compulsively, to the point where it's causing significant problems in someone's life, the function is not to satiate a natural desire but to meet a deeper need. In addiction, the attempt to satiate the deeper need may also be accompanied by cravings and therefore the two can become confused. For example, if someone masturbates every time they feel lonely or bored or angry or sad, after a while they will associate each of those emotions with cravings. Like Pavlov's dogs that salivated every time they heard a bell whether there was food or not, the addict may seek sexual gratification every time they feel a negative emotion whether or not they feel genuine desire.

How addiction starts

The vast majority of people with sex addiction say their problem started under the age of 16 (40.23 per cent) and for some (5.83 per cent) under the age of 10 (www.sexaddictionhelp.co.uk, 2018). The seeds of sex and porn addiction have almost always been sown long before the relationship began, and regrettably for many, a fulfilling relationship is not enough to pull the roots out. This is important for couples to know because it can help to demonstrate that the addiction is no reflection on the relationship. A good relationship can make addiction become dormant for a while, but it won't cure it, which means that, regrettably, it was always only a matter of time before the addiction started again.

Before we go on to look at the different types of addiction and how it starts, it's important to understand that what follows are 'explanations' not 'excuses'. One of the challenges of working with couples is that exploring the root cause can sometimes feel like a cop out. And many partners will rightly say, "That doesn't make it OK" or "He/She may have had a difficult childhood, but they're adult now and they still chose to betray me". Another common observation is that many people experience childhood difficulties but don't become addicted. So why did my partner?

Regrettably, there is no single or simple answer to why anybody develops sex addiction. Understanding how something came to be, whether that's how someone became addicted or how you chose the relationship you're in or the job that you do, is almost always a complex interweaving of many different factors, many of which are dependent on another.

For example, if you're an acclaimed violinist, chances are that your love of music started in early childhood and from an early age you learnt that you had an innate musical talent. Perhaps your parents encouraged you to listen to and play music and your passion was nurtured and your efforts and accomplishments praised. Negative events may have played a role too. Perhaps your first violin was inherited from your late grandfather who you miss very much, but who inspired you to commit to the instrument. If you also had the financial resources to pay for lessons and perhaps go and see live concerts to feed your ambition, and your local secondary school happened to be known for its excellent music teaching, then your journey to success had an excellent start. However, changing just a few key factors or introducing a discriminating wild card such as illness or parental separation might have changed your direction and set you on a very different path. Understanding the fragility of a life path is important because it can help us to understand why people with an almost identical history might develop very differently. It can also help us not to place undue blame or regret on one single incident or circumstance, something that is especially important in sex addiction where shame can play such a crucial role.

When looking at the causes of sex addiction, it's important to ask two questions. The first is, 'why does someone become an addict?' and the second, 'why did they become addicted to porn or sex?' The answers to the first question generally reside in childhood, whereas the answer to the second is usually around the time of puberty and adolescence.

Classifications of sex addiction

Although there are a significant number of characteristics that are common to everyone who develops sex addiction, there are differences in the extent of the addiction and style. Broadly speaking, addiction is trauma-induced, attachment-induced or opportunity-induced, or in some cases, a combination of two or three (Hall, 2018).

As you can see from Figure 2.1, opportunity is present in each of the three classifications of addiction, but in addition, some people also have difficulties with attachment and/or trauma. Some years ago it was believed that all addiction had its roots in either attachment or trauma, but as pornography becomes increasingly prevalent, so do the people who stumble into sex addiction with no prior difficulties.

We'll briefly look at each of the types and how they can get set up in childhood and adolescence, but if you'd like to read up in more detail on sex addiction, do get a copy of *Understanding and Treating*

Figure 2.1 The OAT Classification Model (Hall, 2018)

Sex and Porn Addiction, which focuses specifically on the person with the addiction.

Opportunity-induced addiction

Whatever a person's history and individual circumstances, if there was no opportunity they wouldn't 'act out'. And the reality of the Western world today is that 'opportunity' is everywhere. However, some peoples' brains are more predisposed to take that opportunity if they have a history of addiction (Hall, 2018). As we will see later in this chapter, if people have a history of trauma or attachment difficulties, they are also more likely to get hooked.

Sex is now available anywhere and everywhere – online and offline. Whether you're male, female, queer, straight, gay, bi or anywhere else on a spectrum, you can find anything you desire easily and anonymously. Indeed, you can find a whole load of stuff you don't desire, but get hooked nonetheless. No addiction can exist without opportunity, and in the absence of adequate education and advice, people will experiment and explore and take risks that they didn't know were there. It is the nature of adolescence, when most addictions start, that we like new and pleasurable experiences and which ones we choose to follow and for how long is dependent on our life experiences. We will go on to explore these in a moment, but it's important to highlight that society is responsible for some of the causes of sex and porn addiction, in particular, our policies on Internet pornography and sex education. I am not trying to suggest that we should enforce some kind of sexual prohibition, but in the same way as we teach and encourage healthy eating and responsible drinking, so we should establish appropriate public information for healthy sexuality. Information that allows people to make informed choices rather than blindly stumbling into addiction as so many find they do.

There are some people who are more likely to develop addiction than others, and broadly speaking they are those who also have issues with the following:

- *Developing self-control* – this is particularly relevant for those in adolescence who may have more issues with impulse control or who have not had appropriate boundaries put in place by parents. A family background that has been very rigid and strict is more likely to result in someone who either rebels or finds it difficult to set boundaries for themselves.

- *Managing difficult feelings* – children learn how to express their emotions from watching their parents, which means that people who had poor role models are less likely to know how to appropriately and healthily express themselves. So families where emotions were either kept hidden or were expressed dramatically or dangerously are more likely to foster addiction.

- *Secrets and shame* – shame is the common denominator in almost all addictions, and when a child is brought up to feel shame about themselves, they're more likely to get caught in shame-based issues in adulthood. There is also a correlation between secretive families and addiction, with 41.79 per cent describing this as their experience in the survey undertaken for *Understanding & Treating Sex Addiction* (Hall, 2013). When a child has been brought up to keep secrets, then it is much easier as an adult to live a double life.

- *Poor sex education* – all of us need guidance and education in order to make choices for ourselves. When sex education has been poor or absent this can lead to increased feelings of shame around sex, increased experimentation and poor decision-making.

- *Adolescent loneliness* – using masturbation for comfort is a common and natural pastime for most adolescents, but if a young person feels isolated from others and unable to fit in with peers, they are less likely to develop other coping strategies and learn to turn to people for comfort.

Trauma-induced addiction

The links between trauma and addiction are well known and have been discussed in addiction circles for many years (Carruth, 2011). Addiction may on some occasions be directly triggered by a traumatic event – for example, bereavement, physical assault, sudden illness or witnessing a violent or life-threatening act. Or sometimes a traumatic event or events occur in childhood, and sex becomes a way of coping with the subsequent emotional and physical fallout.

Significant trauma can also have a direct impact on the structure of the brain and the repetitive nature of the compulsive behaviour can become a way of soothing a hyperactive amygdala and limbic system and reduce symptoms of hyper- and hypo-arousal (Fowler, 2006; Fisher, 2007).

Someone with a trauma-induced addiction is most likely to use the behaviour to self-soothe difficult emotions and the chosen behaviour may in some way replicate the initial trauma. There has been increasing evidence that some compulsive fetishes, behaviours and paraphilias are linked to previous trauma. The Opponent Process Theory of Acquired Motivation (Soloman, 1980) describes how a negative emotion or experience can be reframed as a positive in order to re-write the script. For example, someone who was bullied and humiliated as a child might pay a dominatrix to sexually arouse them by doing likewise, hence turning trauma into triumph (Birchard, 2011).

Traumas come in many different shapes and sizes. Some are very obvious, such as violent assaults or childhood abuse, but others are more subtle or may have occurred very early in childhood before language developed and hence be impossible to remember in words. If someone with addiction has experienced any kind of trauma that generated fear, then their addiction is probably linked.

Attachment-induced addiction

'Addiction is an attachment disorder' is a common refrain among addiction specialists and this is undoubtedly true in a significant number of cases (Flores, 2004; Katehakis, 2016). When a child forms a secure attachment with their primary care giver they are more likely to grow into an adult with positive self-esteem who is able to tolerate and manage strong emotions and mild trauma (Potter-Efron, 2006), but if positive parenting has been unreliable or absent, a child is more likely to fear negative feelings and turn to an addiction for comfort during times of trouble rather than to a person.

Someone with an attachment-induced addiction will often be unconsciously using their behaviour as a way of soothing relational pain such as fears of rejection or suffocation, loneliness or low self-esteem. For partners, this can be difficult to understand, especially if your relationship had always been close and loving. Ironically, sex addiction is often used to alleviate fears of losing the relationship, while increasing the likelihood that their fears will be realised.

Healthy attachment starts from the moment we are born. A newborn baby 'attaches' to their primary care giver, usually its mother, in order for survival. As the child grows they continue to need that attachment in order to develop healthily. When a child feels nurtured and cared for they have the courage to explore their world, knowing that safety is just a cry away. This attachment is important for emotional as well as physical development. When a child is still in the pre-verbal stage, they need a parent who is empathically attuned to their needs. And as they learn to talk they need a parent who is encouraging and responsive to their efforts to communicate. Without this a child may not develop the necessary skills to recognise and communicate their needs to others appropriately or to recognise and respond to the needs of others – including sexual needs. However, the effects are not just emotional, they are also biologically imprinted and affect the developing brain (Katehakis, 2016).

Someone who has an attachment-induced addiction is most likely to grow up into someone who has difficulties in their adult relationships. Certain styles of relating can develop and often these play out in the couple's dynamics throughout their time together. There's much more on this in Part II.

How addiction is maintained and reinforced

Now we've looked at how sex addiction begins, it's important to understand how it is maintained and reinforced. Almost all of us will have been attracted to an addictive substance or process at some stage in our lives, but most of us are able to pull back. We recognise within us a point where our indulgence is becoming problematic and we either curtail our habit or stop all together. We know that although we may be enjoying what we're doing, it's either already beginning to harm us or will do at some point in the future.

There are a number of reasons why this doesn't happen for people with an addiction. As we've already explored, this is partly due to brain development and chemistry. The more someone uses a chemical or a process to produce a dopamine high, the less able the brain is to produce sufficient through its own resources, and the more effective the high, the stronger the memory and the brain's orientation towards seeking it again. In addition to this, people with addictions get trapped into a cycle of repetitive behaviour that, until recognised, is impossible to stop. There are a number of different cycles that professionals use. Here, we will look at my six-phase cycle of addiction (Hall, 2018). The length of each phase, and the length of time between each phase, varies from individual to individual, as does the content, but in brief, the cycle revolves as shown in Figure 2.2.

1. *Dormant* – this is the phase where the addiction is temporarily in remission but underlying issues, whether opportunity-, trauma- or attachment-induced, remain unresolved. Life may appear 'normal', but it's simply a matter of time before a trigger occurs.
2. *Trigger* – the trigger is an event, an opportunity, a bodily sensation, emotion or thought process that activates the behaviour. Almost anything may be a trigger, but most commonly it will be a sexual opportunity or a negative emotion such as anxiety, anger, depression, sadness, boredom, loneliness or frustration. There may be a single trigger, but often they are multiple and may be conscious or unconscious.
3. *Preparation* – the preparation phase can vary in length considerably from just a few minutes to open a web page to many weeks of planning an affair. This phase includes practical preparations such as the where, when and how as well as psychological

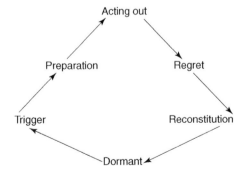

Figure 2.2 The six-phase cycle of addiction (Hall, 2018)

strategies to create the environment where acting out can be tolerated and/or enjoyed.

4. *Acting out* – for some, acting out is a single event such as visiting a sex worker, which may last just a few minutes, whereas for others it may be a week-long binge of pornography use. Some describe it as a highpoint that brings euphoria and relief, but for others the accompanying relief is purely about getting the deed over and done with so they can finally begin their descent back to the comfort of the dormant phase.

5. *Regret* – depending on the consequences of acting out, the impact on personal values and someone's commitment to change, the regret phase may be experienced as little more than a momentary 'oops' or weeks of despair, shame and self-loathing.

6. *Reconstitution* – during the reconstitution phase life is either consciously or unconsciously put back together again. It may be a time for rebuilding self-esteem, covering tracks and/or renewing resolutions not to act out again.

Understanding this cycle of addiction, identifying and personalising each element, is one of the keys to long-term recovery for people with addiction. We will explore this further in the next chapter, but for now, let's look at how you can recognise if this really is sex or porn addiction.

Is it an addiction?

You may be reading this book because you've already confirmed with a professional that the problem is sex or porn addiction, if you haven't what follows can be a start to that process. Professional assessment is essential so that both partners in the couple relationship know what's happening and understand what may lie ahead. If the problem is addiction, then you're reading the right book and you'll find lots more on how to recover as individuals and as a couple. But if the problem is not addiction, then your journey will be a very different one. The questions below should be answered by the person with the addiction.

1. Does your sexual behaviour or porn use have a 'significant' negative impact on other areas of your life, such as maintaining or

forming relationships, spending time with family and friends, concentrating on work or studies, getting into debt, risking your mental or physical health, maintaining personal and legal boundaries?

2. Do you find yourself struggling to concentrate on other areas of your life because you are preoccupied with thoughts and feelings about your porn use or sexual behaviour?

3. Have you noticed that you need more and more stimuli or risk, or that you are watching what you would describe as more extreme porn, in order to achieve the same level of arousal and excitement?

4. Have you tried to limit your porn use or sexual behaviours, or stop all together, but repeatedly failed?

If the answer is 'Yes', to three or more of these questions, then someone is likely to be struggling with sex or porn addiction, but professional assessment should still be sought. A formal assessment will not only confirm a diagnosis of addiction but should also provide a guideline to the severity of the problem. Some people are mildly addicted and some are severely addicted; some have concurrent mental health problems and some are also addicted to other things such as alcohol or drugs. A full assessment can ensure that an appropriate treatment protocol is applied to ensure recovery is secured as quickly as possible. While many people believe they can stop on their own and are tempted not to get professional help, this is can have a particularly negative impact on couple relationships. Partners understandably need to know that the addiction is being taken seriously and the addicted partner is committed to recovery, at whatever cost. But most importantly, remember that addictions are coping strategies and the devastation of the tidal wave will leave many things to cope with. It's true for some that the pain of discovery temporarily makes the addiction feel abhorrent, a bit like the thought of drinking alcohol when you have a hangover. But hangovers wear off, and as a couple you need to know that recovery continues and never rocks your boat again.

References

Birchard, T. (2011) Sexual addiction and the paraphilias. *Sexual Addiction & Compulsivity*, 18: 3.

Blum, K., Braverman, E.R., Holder, J.M., Lubar, J., Monastra, V.J., Miller, D., Laber, J., Chen, T., Comings, E.E. (2000) Reward deficiency syndrome: a biogenetic model for the diagnosis and treatment of impulsive, addictive and compulsive behaviours. *Journal of Psychoactive Drugs*, 32(Suppl): 1–112.

Carnes, P. (1991) *Don't Call It Love: Recovery from sexual addiction.* Bantam: New York.

Carruth, B. (2011) *Psychological Trauma and Addiction Treatment.* Routledge, New York.

Fisher, J. (2007) *Addictions and Trauma Recovery.* New York: Basic Books.

Flores, P.J. (2004) *Addiction as an Attachment Disorder.* Lanham, MD: Aronson.

Fowler, J. (2006) Psychoneurobiology of co-occurring trauma and addictions. *Journal of Chemical Dependency Treatment*, 8(2).

Goodman, A. (1993) Diagnosis and treatment of sexual addiction. *Journal of Sex and Marital Therapy, 19*: 225–251.

Hall, P.A. (2016) *Sex Addiction – The Partner's Perspective.* London: Routledge.

Hall, P.A. (2018) *Understanding & Treating Sex Addiction* (2nd Edition). London: Routledge.

Hilton, D.L. (2013) Pornography addiction: a superanormal stimulus considered in the context of neuroplasticity. *Socioaffective Neuroscience and Psychology*, 3: 20767.

Katehakis, A. (2016) *Sex Addiction as Affect Dysregulation: A neurobiologically informed holistic treatment.* New York: W.W. Norton.

Kuhn, S., Gallinat, J. (2014) Brain structure and functional connectivity associated with pornography consumption: the brain on porn. *Journal of the American Medication Association, Psychiatry 71*(7): 827–834.

Messina, B., Fuentes, D., Tavares, H., Abdo, H.N., Scanavino, M. (2017) Executive functioning of sexually compulsive and non-sexually compulsive men before and after watching an erotic video. *The Journal of Sexual Medicine, 14*(3): 347–354.

Potter-Efron, R. (2006) Attachment, trauma and addiction. In *Psychological Trauma and Addiction Treatment* (edited by B. Carruth). New York: Routledge.

Soloman, R. (1980) The Opponent process theory of acquired motivation. The costs of pleasure and the benefits of pain. *American Psychologist, 35*(8): 691–712.

Stulhofer, A., Jurin, T., Briken, P. (2016) Is high sexual desire a facet of male hypersexuality? Results from an online study. *Journal of Sexual and Marital Therapy, 42*(8): 665–680.

Chapter 3

Prioritising individual recovery

Getting back to dry land

When the tidal wave of addiction has hit your relation-ship, the first thing you need to do is get yourself to safety. While many couples find themselves desperate to make a decision about the future of the relationship, neither partner can do this until they know they're not going to drown. Making a decision that could impact the rest of your life, and certainly your children's lives, is most wisely taken when you both know you are back on solid ground.

The early stages of recovery are the point at which each of you must take individual responsibility for getting yourself to shore. However, that does not mean that you abandon your relation-ship altogether. Some couples hope they can complete the whole journey together, but as you'll see in this chapter, that is often a dangerous approach. Most couples benefit from couple counselling as soon as possible, to ensure their relation-ship doesn't sink while working on their individual recovery, but this does not replace the work you need to do alone. The recovery journey for a partner is very different from that of the person with the addiction and in this chapter we will explore what each of those journeys entail.

The dangers of trying to recover together

There are many admirable reasons why couples want to work through the impact of sex or porn addiction together, but in the early stages this presents many dangers and may impede long-term recovery for each and for the relationship. The trauma of the tidal wave can leave each partner desperately clinging on to the relation-ship, desperate to save it and terrified of being swept away. This is a very natural trauma response as we try to rescue whatever has brought us comfort and security in the past. However, the reality is that the relationship is broken and clinging onto the wreckage can get in the way of rebuilding a more solid and secure relationship and increases the risk of drowning.

Another common reason why many couples want to work through addiction together is because they love each other and want to be part of each other's recovery, but the best way to do that is to ensure that you are in a strong place yourself first. If you've ever been on an aeroplane you'll have heard the safety announcement telling you to put on your own oxygen mask before helping others. No doubt this advice has come from years of experience of knowing that the best intentions of others are not always in the best interest of others. And in my experience, the best safety advice for couples who want to recover from sex addiction is to prioritise your own recovery.

Partners often find it particularly difficult if they feel they're not involved in the addicted partner's journey. They fear that the addicted partner will blame the relationship or fail to share the full story, or indeed, that they will share the whole story with someone else and they'll be left never knowing the truth. When trust has been so devastatingly violated, this is understandable, and hence clear communication about individual recovery journeys should be established, but my experience has taught me that even in situations where the addicted partner is committed to being 100 per cent honest and open they're simply unable to do so within couple counselling until they've established some level of individual recovery. The bottom line is that no-one can be honest with their partner or explain what they've done until they're able to be honest with themselves. The nature of addiction is that it's used to escape reality, hence establishing what reality is rarely happens overnight. A full disclosure is an important part of the recovery journey for couples, but before this is undertaken the addicted partner needs to understand that telling the truth is more important than saving the relationship and they cannot control the outcome of honesty. In addition, partners need to be equipped and feel confident enough that they will cope with whatever the truth may be.

Individual recovery is also important because the needs of couples are very different at this early stage and it's almost impossible to ensure that both partners get their needs met adequately and effectively in joint therapy. Partners need the space to be heard with compassion and empathy, to have their feelings validated and to be reassured that the addiction is not their fault, while helping them to manage the roller coaster of emotions they're experiencing. The addicted partner needs to feel safe enough to share their story completely, which means having a space that is free from judgement, shame and immediate consequence, and to be challenged to look beyond what might initially be superficial explanations for their behaviour and establish recovery techniques. Both also benefit enormously from developing connections with peer groups who can provide independent support and encouragement for many years to come. Working together as a couple is essential to ensure neither partner experiences further damage, as well as to save the relationship, or to healthily separate. We will cover the principles of that work in the next chapter, but that work does not replace individual recovery.

Finally, individual recovery is also essential to provide the recovery space for meaning to be developed. The addicted partner needs to fully understand why they developed an addiction and why they betrayed for so long so they can share this with their partner. Without this knowledge, rebuilding trust is impossible. Similarly, partners need individual space to understand what's happened to them, a space where they can develop a sense of safety and stability on their own; a place to rebuild their self-esteem and trust in themselves.

There are, of course, always exceptions, and no doubt some couples have successfully recovered from sex addiction together, but the risks are great and simply not worth taking. Regrettably, some well-meaning couple counsellors try to establish recovery through couple work and it may be years later that the discovery is made that the relation-ship still has a hole in its hull or that there are still secrets in the hold. To ensure this doesn't happen to you, I recommend you take the safety advice and first put on 'your' oxygen mask.

The partner's journey

There is not room in this book to fully explore the extensive and important needs of partners who find themselves the innocent victims of sex or porn addiction. You can find much, much more about partner recovery in *Sex Addiction – The Partner's Perspective* (Hall, 2016), but here we'll outline what those needs are and how they can help partners get back to the safety of dry land. In brief, recovery means learning to SURF. The acrostic SURF comes from the well-known saying by mindfulness guru, Jon Kabat-Zinn "You can't stop the waves, but you can learn to surf". In other words, while there may be a roller coaster of turbulent emotions that you have little control over, some of which will regrettably be triggered by further disclosures or discoveries, you can develop strategies to keep your head above water. I use SURF as an acrostic to remember the key stages of recovery for partners:

S – survive the trauma

Nothing prepares you for the discovery of sex addiction – absolutely nothing. The overwhelming first emotion experienced by almost every partner is shock. Even those who have been suspicious for a while are ill-prepared for the devastation of full disclosure, or discovery. Once the numbness of shock has worn off, many partners experience a flood of emotions that can feel totally overwhelming and for many the first six months are a roller-coaster ride of intense emotional pain, and little can be done except hang on. The most common feelings experienced can be grouped under seven broad emotional categories: shock, anger, grief, fear, shame, disgust, and for a few, relief. These emotions can seem to come from nowhere and many partners describe feeling ambushed by these feelings and struggling to cope with everyday life.

There has been increasing awareness over recent years that the emotional responses of partners are similar to those who have experienced trauma (Steffens & Rennie, 2007) such as a sudden bereavement or assault. This is often referred to now as 'relational trauma' with some partners developing PTSD (post-traumatic stress disorder) symptoms which would almost certainly require additional trauma support from a health professional.

In addition to the onslaught of painful emotions, most partners also find themselves plagued by questions that seem to demand an immediate answer. Questions such as 'what should I do?', 'who do I tell?', 'do I know everything?' and perhaps the most painful one, 'why did you do this?' These questions all come from a place of wanting safety and stability, something that can only ultimately be found within yourself, namely by developing self-care and emotional resilience.

U – understand the cycle of reaction

After approximately six months, most partners will have developed a greater sense of stability and safety and feel that they have survived the trauma. Many feel scarred and battle weary, but they have survived. However, like the cycle of addiction, many partners find themselves also trapped in an unwanted and repeating cycle – the cycle of reaction, as you can see in Figure 3.1. One minute they feel as though they can cope and are beginning to make sense of what's happened and get themselves back together again, then bang – they're back to square one again. This cycle is explored in depth in my partner book, but we'll look at each element in brief here.

Like those with an addiction, partners can have periods of time when they are dormant and feel in control of their emotional responses, but within this cycle that dormant phase contains the partner's history, some of which may be unconsciously continuing

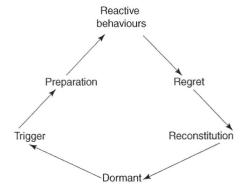

Figure 3.1 The Cycle of Reaction (Hall, 2016)

the cycle. Like the person with the addiction, partners also have triggers. A trigger might be something significant like discovering a new piece of information that had been withheld, or it may be hearing a news item on prostitution or seeing an attractive person in the street. Once triggered, partners enter a preparation phase where negative thoughts fuel the emotional trigger and the feelings of fear, anger or despair can grow. In the reactive behaviour phase of the cycle, partners feel they have no control of their thoughts, feelings or behaviour. For some partners that might be an angry outburst; for others it could be a self-harming strategy such as binging on food or drink; for others it might be a panic attack or depression. As this dissipates many partners feel sadness and regret that they have found themselves, yet again, unable to control their reaction to a trigger. During the reconstitution phase, partners engage in a range of self-soothing strategies which can help them to feel safe again, but unless time is spent exploring unresolved issues of the dormant phase it may simply be a matter of time before they're triggered again.

Like any repeating cycle, once the stages have been identified it can be much easier to develop strategies to get off the cycle. For partners that means recognising and avoiding triggers, if possible, and developing healthy self-care strategies for unavoidable triggers. It also means challenging their own cognitive distortions and self-limiting beliefs and developing positive emotional reactions that they feel comfortable and confident with.

R – repair self-identity and self-esteem

Perhaps the most damaging impact of sex and porn addiction is what it does to a partner's sense of self. The term ego-fragmentation (Minwalla, 2018) has been used to describe the effect that long-term deceit and betrayal can have on a partner's sense of a solid and whole identity. This goes much deeper than simply impacting self-esteem and self-confidence, but to the core of knowing who we are. When your world has been turned upside down and inside out, an identity crisis is common and hence partners need space to focus on re-establishing who they are and how they function in the world.

An essential part of this recovery journey is being able to see yourself as someone independent from the relationship. Someone who can be confident and content in life, whether single or in a relationship. It is only by establishing this that confidence can be gained that rebuilding the shattered relationship is coming from a place of positive choice rather than a wounded need. It also helps to establish confidence that if the relationship breaks down in the future, perhaps because of a relapse, you would cope.

F – face the future

The future for partners is always changed by addiction, not just in terms of the future of the relationship, but also the impact on family members, friendships and lifestyle. Partners have choices, tough ones and ones they never wanted to have, but nonetheless they are choices. For some the future means staying together and rebuilding the relationship, for others it means separation and having to work out how to co-parent and whether to embark on a new relationship. For all there will be inevitable lifestyle changes, perhaps moving home, changing jobs, renegotiating friendships and extended family relationships, taking up new hobbies and health and fitness routines. There is a cost to staying in a relationship and a cost to leaving, and for most partners these calculations are simpler to evaluate alone, but either way, recognising that you continue to have choices and can rebuild a life that is meaningful and rewarding is a key intervention for long-term partner recovery.

The addicted partner's journey

While stopping acting out might be instantaneous, recovery is a process that takes much, much longer and it's a journey that an addicted partner has to be willing to undertake for life. In the same way as we don't have space here to cover the partner journey, we don't have space for addiction recovery either. You'll find everything you need in the companion book, *Understanding and Treating Sex and Pornography Addiction* (Hall, 2018), but in the meantime let me introduce you to another acrostic – CHOICE.

The CHOICE Recovery Model is more than a treatment plan, it's a philosophy; it's more than a strategy for grudgingly stopping compulsive behaviours, but a roadmap to establish confident recovery and a new way of life. The CHOICE stages of recovery are as follows.

C – challenge core beliefs

There are only two reasons why human beings ever change. Either the pain of staying the same is so great that they have to change, or they have a vision of something better. Change is a 'choice', but before you can make that choice you have to root out any faulty core beliefs and thinking patterns that might block change. There are many different core beliefs that block recovery, but broadly speaking, they all fall under three headings: 'I don't need to change', 'I don't want to change' and 'I can't change'. If you're reading this book then it's unlikely you fall under the first heading, but you may not be fully aware of the extent of change that is required when we give up an addiction.

Undoubtedly the biggest block to change comes from the faulty core beliefs that leave us feeling shame, such as believing that you're fundamentally a bad person or defective in some way. Shame thrives in secrecy and often it is not until shame is brought into the light that it can be truly dealt with. Many people with addiction are not initially aware of their damaging core beliefs because the addiction has successfully anaesthetised it, but as the anaesthetic wears off in recovery, it will become more and more apparent and the need for fundamental change will be recognised.

H – have a vision

There are two ways of looking at addiction recovery: either you can see it as giving something up, or you can see it as starting something new. Both are of course true and it's a choice whether to focus on the losses or the gains; to look at the past or the future. Committing to recovery requires changing negative core beliefs and developing a vision of a new, happier future; a future that is free of shame and which offers fulfilment. Inevitably there will be a mourning period for what has been lost, but as long as there is true hope for the future, the loss process can be made bearable. To secure recovery, you need to have a vision for life that will replace the addiction and provide motivation for change, even when recovery feels tough. And for those in relationships, that vision has to be viable whether the relationship survives or not.

Another key element of building a vision of the future is that it is based on a secure personal value system. Addiction robs people of their values as they see themselves behaving in ways that are against what they hold dear. Re-establishing values gives a sense of meaning and purpose in life that can cement a commitment to recovery and a life without addiction.

O – overcome compulsive behaviours

It may seem strange to some readers that this is not the first step in recovery, but in my experience many people with addiction struggle to stop acting out until they've confronted any self-limiting core beliefs and have found a motivation for change. For those in couple relationships, saving the relationship is a core driver for recovery, but partners need to know that the addicted partner wants to recover for themselves, not just to save the relationship. What's more, partners need to be confident that recovery is now recognised as a positive choice, not something that has been reluctantly undertaken because they've been caught.

In order to overcome compulsive behaviours it's essential that each person understands their individual cycle of addiction and the unique factors that keep them trapped in their behaviour. Back in Chapter 1, I introduced you to the six-phase model that I use in my recovery courses, and like partners, the addicted partner needs to personalise their cycle and develop strategies for ending it.

I – identify positive sexuality

Being in recovery means giving up addiction, not giving up sex, so identifying what positive, non-compulsive sexuality means is essential for long-term success. We talk much more about rebuilding sexuality as a couple in Chapter 14, but it's in individual recovery where the foundations are put in place. Everyone in recovery needs to first determine for themselves what positive sexuality means to them and what boundaries they need to put in place to ensure they can begin to enjoy their sexuality in a fulfilling and healthy way. It will take time for old habits to change, psychologically and physically, but I'm pleased to say that there are many hundreds of men and women in recovery who enjoy sex more now than they ever did during their addiction.

C – connect with others

The irony of addictive behaviours is that they are so often used to ease the pain of loneliness and isolation, but they actually create more. The secrecy and shame of being dependent on porn, betraying a loved one, or only being able to have sex when drunk or high on drugs results in avoiding intimacy rather than creating it and nurturing it. When we can connect with others and build relationships where our relational needs are met, not only can we feel supported in recovery, but we begin to heal the wounds that cause and maintain the addiction.

Connecting with others is equally important for those in couple relationships as it is for those who are single and includes building relationships with friends and extended family, not just with a partner. It's not possible for any human being to meet all the needs of another, whether that's recreational needs or emotional support. Furthermore, it's understandable that a partner may not be able to provide the understanding, empathy and encouragement required for recovery, and hence being part of a recovery community is also a key element of overcoming the addiction.

E – establish confident recovery

Recovery is not about what you 'give up', but what you 'take up', and establishing confident long-term recovery means developing strategies to avoid slips and relapses and creating a life where being in recovery is something to be enjoyed, rather than endured. Those strategies will include daily disciplines to strengthen recovery and avoid relapse and also healthy pursuits and pastimes. Some of those pastimes can be enjoyed as a couple, but it's also important to find ways to enjoy quality alone time as well as building relationships with others.

Before we end this chapter I want to add another reason why individual recovery comes first, a reason that has caused great confusion and harm to partners: co-dependency. Co-dependency is a clumsy and damaging label, and while it's still commonly used within chemical addiction, it is meaningless in sex and porn addiction. Co-dependency is an umbrella heading for any kind of relationship collusion, and as couple therapists know, conscious and unconscious collusions are normal, and often healthy within intimate relationships. For example, a healthy conscious collusion might be that one partner is responsible for finance because they're better with figures than the other, while the other will be responsible for their social life because making friends is one of their strengths. Whether you have consciously or unconsciously agreed that you will care for each other during difficult times, that is a healthy collusion, it is not a sign that either of you are co-dependent.

I am absolutely delighted that since writing the first edition of *Understanding & Treating Sex Addiction* in 2012, the automatic labelling of partners as co-dependent has mostly disappeared and instead a relational trauma model has taken its place. However, in some situations, couples have unconsciously colluded with each other in relational factors that have impeded relationship growth, such as avoiding talking about difficult issues or becoming enmeshed or distant. This seems to be particularly apparent in couples where either or both partners experienced attachment difficulties or trauma in childhood. In these cases, the couple relationship will often have been plagued with problems around intimacy and trust for many years, and for the relationship to be repaired, each must own the impact of their past through individual therapy where they can feel free to be open without fear of judgement or negative reactions. If we go back to our boat metaphor, this is a scenario where each crewmember, knowingly or unknowingly, had brought something on board the relation-ship that has been slowly eroding the hold. These potentially dangerous items need to be uncovered and let go before any kind of relation-ship can be rebuilt, whether that's together or with someone else in the future.

References

Hall, P.A. (2016) *Sex Addiction – The Partner's Perspective.* London: Routledge.
Hall, P.A. (2018) *Understanding and Treating Sex and Pornography Addiction* (2nd Edition). London: Routledge.

Minwalla, O. (2018). Thirteen dimensions of sex addiction-induced trauma (SAIT) among partners and spouses impacted by sex addiction. Retrieved from the Institute for Sexual Health, 20 May 2018. https://theinstituteforsexualhealth.com/thirteen-dimensions-of-sex-addiction-induced-trauma-sait-among-partners-and-spouses-impacted-by-sex-addiction/

Steffens, B., Rennie, R. (2007) The traumatic nature of disclosure for wives of sexual addicts. *Sexual Addiction and Compulsivity. The Journal of Treatment and Prevention*, *13*: 247–267.

Chapter 4

Surviving the impact stage

The first stage for every couple relationship is about surviving the impact of the tidal wave. This stage is all about damage control and most commonly lasts between three and six months. The tidal wave has hit and the task is to get each of you, and what's left of your relation-ship, back to solid ground without doing any further harm to either of you on the journey. In the last chapter we focused on what you needed to do as individuals to get back to safety, and in this chapter we will focus on what you need to do as a couple. In this chapter I will also introduce you to some of the couples who kindly shared their experience in the couple survey; what helped them in the first six months and also what hindered them.

Every couple is of course different as is each situation that they have to face, and that means that timescales will vary too. Some couples find they can navigate back to shore quicker than others and this will largely depend on how strong your relationship was before the tidal wave hit, how big the tidal wave was and how strong each of you are as swimmers. During this impact stage, emotions are running high and many people find themselves thinking and behaving erratically and uncharacteristically (Baucom et al., 2011). The most important thing is to take your time and to understand that, before you can make decisions about the future of your relationship, you need to be in recovery from the addiction and have survived the trauma of discovery or disclosure.

Many partners are keen to receive a full disclosure as quickly as possible, but as we saw in the last chapter, this is often ineffective at best, damaging at worse, until both have established at least some individual recovery. We will talk further about disclosure in the next chapter, but for now we'll look at the key tasks for this first stage of your journey as a couple.

The tasks

The tasks of the impact stage incorporate the benefits of the dual process model of coping with loss (Stroebe & Schut, 1999). This model, which emphasises the importance of focusing attention on restoration, as well as loss, demonstrates that healthy grief work means oscillating between loss-orientated and restoration-orientated coping activities. We will look at each of these in more depth over the coming pages, but in brief the tasks for the impact stage are:

1. *Commit to self-care* – part of this will be your individual recovery journey, but will also include taking responsibility for your general physical and emotional health.
2. *Look after family* – if you have children or are responsible for extended family members then you'll need to agree together what will be shared about your situation and agree how to protect those you love from the repercussions.
3. *Establish accountability* – this is the first step in rebuilding trust which we will look at in a lot more depth in Chapter 13, but in the first six months accountability will help you to ensure that both you as individuals, and your relationship, aren't damaged any further.
4. *Minimise conflict* – angry feelings are very natural and normal when there's been any kind of relational trauma, but learning to share those feelings in a healthy way can help to protect yourselves and your relationship.
5. *Agree 'check-ins'* – 'check-ins' are the term commonly used for allotted times when you will talk about what's happened and what you're each going through. Agreeing these times will not only help you to share information and feelings on a regular basis, but can also help to protect other time for trying to live a 'normal' life.

I. Commit to self-care

When we're under stress it's easy to forget to look after ourselves; to start eating junk food, drink too much, give up on exercise routines and either sleep too much or hardly at all. But we all know that when we're struggling emotionally, that's when we have to make even more effort to look after ourselves physically. Physical self-care in the wake of sex addiction also means that it's imperative to see a sexual health professional to check if either of you has contracted an STI (sexually transmitted infection). In addition to physical self-care, looking after yourself emotionally is also important. That means making time to engage in activities that you find relaxing and enjoy, whether that's reading a book, watching a movie or going out for a walk. Some couples are able to continue to do some of these things together, while others find it easier to relax when the other one isn't around.

Many couples will wonder if time apart will be helpful either for both or one of them. In the survey, all of the partners said that they found space apart beneficial and one regretted she had not taken more. There are no hard or fast rules on this, but many couples do say that a period of separation gives them space to focus on their own needs. That could be just a few weeks or months, or coming to an agreement that you will have time apart at weekends or some evenings. This latter arrangement often works well for couples with children who don't want to disrupt routines or cause alarm. Most couples agree to having separate bedrooms if possible, and both benefit from carving out more alone time for reading recovery litera-ture, individual therapy or group work with other addicts and part-ners, or for practising mindfulness, which is a great way to relax and develop the discipline of staying in the moment rather than dwelling on the past or worrying about the future.

Self-care is different for all of us, but however you do it, the commitment is not just to help you to recover quicker, but also to give you more strength for coping with other commitments such as work and family. If either of you is struggling with self-care then it's important to see a health professional to establish if medical inter-vention such as a course of anti-depressants would help.

2. Look after family

Most of the couples who undertook the survey for this book had children, stepchildren or grandchildren. The ages varied hugely, but all agreed that it was important to both of them to protect them from too much information and keep family routines as familiar as possible, at least during the first six months. However, some family situations can feel particularly difficult, or even traumatic, such as if you have a wedding to attend or Christmas is on the horizon. You may find talking through these situations with a counsellor beneficial, in part to talk through the emotional impact, but also to explore options for how one or both of you might be able to separate yourself from the proceedings. Some couples agree to telling white lies, such as an unplanned business trip or illness so you don't feel you have to play 'happy families' when your life feels like it's falling apart, but when there have already been so many lies, telling more can feel very uncomfortable.

Many partners understandably feel angry that they have to keep a secret from those they love, or lie directly to avoid suspicions or disclosure. It's important to remember that this is not a long-term strategy and your reasons for doing this are to protect family members, not to protect the addicted partner. We will explore further 'who to tell' in Chapter 5, but one partner advises "choose carefully who you tell about what you have discovered or been told – what is said cannot be unsaid and there is life to be lived afterwards". This is good advice during the first six months, when feelings of anger or desperation can cloud our decision-making ability and stop us thinking about the long-term consequences, consequences that everyone will have to live with.

3. Establish accountability

All of the couples cited accountability as one of the most beneficial things they did during the first six months, although most of the partners warned that dishonesty continued after this period, whether that was about the past or about current behaviour. One partner says, "Don't expect absolute honesty during the first 6 months while he's still getting into recovery". Another partner said, "Put an accountability contract in place straight away, but don't expect complete total honesty – continued drip drip disclosures".

The purpose of an accountability contract is threefold. For the partner it can provide a greater level of reassurance that the compulsive behaviour has stopped, which will help to reduce feelings of hypervigilance and the desire to constantly check-up on the addicted partner. For the addicted partner it provides an essential element of relapse prevention, because acting out is much harder to deny or hide and it can begin to reduce shame as a new level of honesty and integrity is found. One addicted partner in the survey put it like this:

> The more accountability you can provide the better. My experience is that being proactive in the provision of information and not allowing blind spots to develop is very helpful. From an addict perspective the proactive nature of this is very helpful in building one's own self trust and esteem. I feel better about myself in taking ownership and behaving like an adult who knows that the responsibility for this rebuilding lies with me. Finding things to feel better about is a real problem for an addict, not least because the shame of acting out makes one feel that you should never feel good. This proactive behaviour is a good beginning in rebuilding my life.

Finally, an accountability contract benefits the relationship by minimising unnecessary suspicion, anxiety and conflict. In my experience, a significant number of acrimonious couple interactions can be avoided by establishing an accountability contract and, crucially, much of the ongoing trauma that partners experience can be eliminated. This is especially true when the contract is mutually devised and each partner fully understands the agreement they are making and their responsibility for upholding it.

Before creating your accountability contract you need to have agreed that all previous acting out contacts and websites and any other paraphernalia have been deleted or disposed of. That means that any Internet device has been cleaned of past behaviours including photos, chat history, any receipts or payments, website history and contacts. You should also put down in writing what you are each agreeing to avoid any miscommunication or doubt in the future. The areas of accountability that you need to consider are:

- *Technology use* – including the television and anything linked to the Internet, such as laptops, tablets, mobile phones and gaming consoles. Also social media such as Twitter, LinkedIn and Facebook. Either unlock any passwords or make sure they're known by both of you. You can also install a porn blocker and a tracker which will detail sites that have been visited. Agree that nothing will be deleted and agree an open technology policy, meaning that partners can look at any device any time they feel in need of reassurance. You could also agree that no Internet device will be used at home by the addicted partner unless you are both in the same room and devices such as tablets and mobile phones are left visible and not on silent. The only exception to this policy may be when someone works from home or when taking confidential calls and messages from others in recovery.

- *Finance* – if money has been spent on acting out then all bank account statements should be available online or on paper for both partners to see. Also consider agreeing maximum cash withdrawals and no purchases without a receipt beyond a certain amount. For example, you might agree that £30 a week on incidentals such as coffees and drinks is OK without a receipt, but any single purchase above £10 should be accompanied by a receipt. It's also wise to agree no 'surprise' purchases, for example presents, as the very nature of a surprise is that it needs to be hidden for a while and this is often very triggering for partners. Also agree to itemised phone bills, both landline and mobile, and access to work expenses and work credit card statements.

- *Social events* – this includes anything where both of you are going and social events that the addicted partner may go to alone. The most important thing is to plan ahead, make sure dates and times are in diaries and you know in advance who will be there. If it's a joint social event, agree before you go how you will get away early if either of you feels you're not coping, or at least how you might be able to get time out if required. For many couples it's also helpful to agree what alcohol consumption will be acceptable at the event and if the addicted partner is out alone, often it's agreed that there will be no drinking and staying away overnight is not an option in the first six months.

- *Alone time* – as mentioned earlier, space is something that every couple said was helpful in the first six months. Like social time, plan ahead on who will be where, when and doing what.

- *Work* – work time can be especially triggering for partners as it's so much harder to keep track of where each other is and what you're doing. How you manage this will depend on your individual work commitments, but should include access to the work diary and regular contact during the day. If travel requires working away then many couples agree to do whatever is in their power to avoid overnight stays, even if that means getting a 4.00 am flight or turning down invitations to conferences or job opportunities. Remember this is not an agreement that has to last the rest of your lives, but a short-term strategy to help you both find some stability for your relationship.

- *Recovery activities* – both partners and addicted partners should be regularly engaged in some kind of recovery activity, whether that's individual therapy, being a member of a support group, attending 12-Step fellowships and/or doing step work and therapy homework. If possible, try to establish routines of what's attended, where and when and agree that you will discuss your individual journeys in your check-in sessions that we'll discuss later in this section.

Before we end this section on establishing accountability, let me offer a few more tips that can save you both a lot of heartache. Firstly, start using video calls rather than making a standard voice call, as this will prove the addicted partner is phoning from where they say they are. Allow extra time for any kind of travel and if you are going to be late, always video call as soon as possible to explain. For both of these to work you also need to ensure you charge your phone regularly – many couples have had easily avoidable rows because one of them had run out of charge and hence couldn't make or receive a call. Consider activating 'find my phone' and putting a tracker on the addicted partner's car – again, this can avoid a lot of unnecessary conflict over where you are. Please be aware neither of these are foolproof and geo-locate does occasionally make mistakes. Another helpful tip is to create what's known as a T-30 diary (Arterburn & Martinkus, 2014). We'll look more at this in Chapter 13, but basically it's a very simple spreadsheet that lists on a day-by-day basis how time will be spent in 30 minute increments. It sounds arduous, but do have a look at Chapter 13 now if you want to see how simple it is. Finally, and perhaps most importantly, be proactive in accountability. Many addicted partners complain that they feel monitored and controlled, and partners complain that they feel forced to act like the police or a parent. But when you have jointly collaborated on your accountability contract and the addicted partner is proactive in offering information, putting receipts and statements in the allocated place, leaving their phone on the side rather than in their pocket, then many of these feelings can be avoided. Furthermore, accountability benefits 'both' of you as individuals as partners feel reassured and the addicted partner will have even more reason to avoid temptations – and it can save your relationship from a lot of unnecessary heartache.

4. Minimise conflict

While anger is natural, unfortunately it can also be a very destructive emotion if it's not managed in a healthy way, and the destruction isn't limited to the person on the receiving end of anger, but on the angry person themselves. Anger floods our body with chemicals that can result not only in a permanent psychological feeling of restlessness and hypervigilance, but it can also result in health issues such as high blood pressure, headaches, stomach problems and a lowered immune system. Sometimes anger is expressed overtly as rage, with obvious signs such as shouting and physical aggression, using abusive language and being spiteful, punishing or making threats. Or anger may be expressed as passive aggression, provoking an argument, being silent or making sly digs or using sarcasm. Sometimes anger is turned inwards, which can lead to self-harming, whether that's physical such as cutting, taking unnecessary risks to personal safety or drinking too much, or emotionally through constant self-criticism and blame.

Agree to have nights off

To minimise conflict and further damage to yourselves as individuals, and your relationship, agree that you will not talk about anything to do with the addiction and what's happened to your relationship before 7.00 am in the morning and after 10.00 am at night, or when you've been drinking alcohol. Emotions run high when we're tired or inebriated and common sense can go out of the window, so only talk when you're both able to be fully present.

Both addicted partners and partners are likely to find themselves struggling with anger during the impact stage, but it may be
expressed in quite different ways. For some couples, anger may have
been an issue within their relationship long before the addiction was
discovered or disclosed, or it may be something that their relationship has never had to face. Conflict is commonplace where there is
anger and it may be something that neither of you have developed
the skills to manage, or indeed something that you've unconsciously
colluded to avoid.

It's important to understand that anger is a healthy emotion; it's
an emotion that helps us protect ourselves and fight for safety and
security. Anger can be a positive and constructive force that can help
you to resolve difficulties and negotiate your needs, but only when it's
communicated assertively rather than aggressively. What follows is
not advice on avoiding anger, but rather minimising the destruction
it can cause to each of you as individuals and the relationship.

- *Identify the anger* – if you notice that you're constantly replaying
  something negative or irritating about your partner in your head,
  or you're repeatedly contradicting or questioning your partner on
  something relatively trivial, or you're becoming irritated with other
  people or routine tasks, then chances are that anger is building.
  And if you're a partner witnessing this in the other, especially if
  eye contact is also being avoided, then an argument is probably
  on the horizon. The sooner one or both of you can identify that
  anger is building the easier it will be to stop it in its tracks.
- *Name the anger* – as soon as one of you has noticed anger
  building, name it. If you're the one feeling angry, acknowledge
  your feelings and if possible explain what has caused it in a
  non-accusatory way to avoid escalation or defensiveness. For
  example, say "I feel angry because you were late and didn't telephone which I feel was thoughtless of you" rather than "You've
  made me angry because you didn't bother to tell me you were
  going to be late". This will be much easier to do if you say it early
  rather than dwelling on it. If you're a partner and you suspect
  your partner is angry, enquire compassionately. In other words,
  saying "it feels as though you're angry about something" will be
  much less antagonistic than "are you angry again?"

- *Discuss the issue* – if the timing's appropriate then talk about what has happened immediately. If it's not, for example if it's very late at night, in public or when you're likely to be interrupted, then agree a time when you will talk. If either of you feels too angry to talk constructively, then agree to have 'time out' and postpone until you've had time to de-escalate your emotions and become more relaxed, using self-care strategies that you will hopefully be developing through your individual recovery. If you agree to 'time out' then agree how long you need, I would suggest at least 30 minutes, and during that time you each agree to take responsibility for reducing your angry feelings rather than replaying negative thoughts in your head. If repeated time outs don't seem to be working, then you could agree to have a ventilation session to clear the air before you discuss the issue. There's much more on constructive communication in Chapter 7 and you'll find further reading in the Resources section at the end of this book.

Ventilation sessions

Sometimes, keeping anger inside feels impossible and one or both of you may feel that you need to share what's going on. The aim of a ventilation session is to get difficult feelings off your chest, not to resolve an issue, and it's important that you both recognise that. The objective is simply to let off steam as safely as possible and postpone discussion to another time. First you'll need to find between 30 and 40 minutes when you won't be interrupted or overheard. The person with the strong emotion has the first 20 minutes to share how they're feeling without interruption. At the end of the 20 minutes, the other has 10–20 minutes to acknowledge what they've heard and share how they feel. When you've each had your allotted time you agree that you will each have some space alone to process what's been said and relax before calmly talking about any issues raised on another occasion. Ventilation sessions require a degree of self-discipline to not respond, or demand a response from the other. Remember, the objective is to clear the air to enable a more constructive conversation to happen at a later date.

Before we end this section on conflict, it needs to be stated that some people find it especially difficult to control their anger and for some couples it can quickly escalate to threats and incidence of verbal or physical abuse. If this is happening for you then it's essential that you seek professional couples therapy immediately to ensure the safety of you both.

5. Agree check-ins

There are two key reasons why regular check-ins are important in the first six months. The first is that they ensure you make the time to talk about what's happened and share the progress that you're making in recovery. Secondly, it ensures you have time when you know you 'won't' talk about it. Many couples make the mistake of either avoiding any conversation about what you're going through or talking about it all the time, neither of which is helpful. You each need to have time when you can try to live a 'normal' life, knowing that the other isn't going to ambush you into a conversation you're not ready to have. Of course, I know life isn't normal and part of the significant loss that partners face is that what they previously thought was 'normal' wasn't what it appeared to be. Nonetheless, by agreeing times when you will talk you allow yourselves space to relax and enjoy other parts of your life, such as time together as a family or simply preparing and eating a meal or watching the TV.

Effective check-in sessions will help both of you to recognise and understand what the other is thinking and feeling, which will help to alleviate insecurity and second-guessing, and also provide a framework for sharing essential practical information. The timing of check-ins will vary from couple to couple depending on your individual circumstances and other commitments, but I would recommend at least two check-ins per week. One should focus on practical information sharing and the other on sharing thoughts and feelings. It's always better to start off with too many sessions in the diary at first than too few. So if you find you often don't have much to say then you can reduce the frequency. However many you have, they should be time-limited, a maximum of 60 minutes, and agreed upon in advance. Below you will find an outline of the proposed content for these sessions which you can follow and there's much more on communication strategies in Chapter 7.

Practical check-in

This is your opportunity to share practical information about your own recovery journey and to request practical changes from your partner that could help your individual journey and your time together or as a family. You may start with sharing what you have done since the last session on your recovery, such as going to meetings, reading literature, doing mindfulness or mediation exercises and other self-care strategies. The other partner may ask questions for clarification, but remember your individual recovery is your responsibility. You can also use this session to highlight any triggers that you've been struggling with and practical strategies you may have to avoid them in the future. This is especially important if it's a trigger that happens within the couple environment, such as a particular TV show or place that you went together. If there are any practical difficulties in the accountability contract, this is also the opportunity to discuss those. End your session thinking about anything that may come up before your next check-in that you would like your partner's support in and also use the time to share anything your partner has done since the last check-in that you have found beneficial.

Emotional check-in

This session should be on a separate occasion to your practical check in and the focus of this is to share your thoughts and feelings. An emotional check-in works best when you agree to take it in turns, with one speaking and the other listening; see Chapter 7 for more communication tips. The objective of an emotional check-in is for each of you to have the opportunity to share what you've been thinking and feeling since your last check-in, in a way that your partner can hear and understand, without becoming defensive or angry. It is not a time to make decisions or expect to find answers, but simply to gain more insight into each other and get feelings off your chest. Some couples toss a coin to agree who will go first, others alternate between each session. Most find it helpful to take notes between sessions of things they want to say and this habit can also help to protect the time between check-ins. If emotions are running very high, some people write down their thoughts and feelings in a letter and use the check-in to read it out. Emotional check-ins can often feel quite draining so make sure you give yourself time afterwards to look after yourself before you have to engage in any other activities. Like ventilation sessions, they require a degree of self-discipline to stick to the guidelines and the allotted time.

The five tasks we have explored in this chapter can help you individually, and as a couple, to survive the first six months and ensure no further damage is done to your relation-ship. Some of it may sound tedious, arduous and even unnatural, but remember the objective is keep you safe and put you both in a stronger position to make longer-term decisions about your relationship. Many of these tasks are ones that you may wish to continue, although you may find yourselves not needing to be quite as strict as some of the strategies and techniques discussed become habit and routine. In a moment we will move on to Part II of this book, where we'll begin to explore the full extent of the damage your relationship has suffered as a result of the compulsive sexual behaviours, but first I'll leave you with some further advice from the couples who have first-hand experience of how difficult the first six months can be.

> Hang in there. Your world is shattered but it can be put back together. Remember your own mistakes. Do not judge and try to forgive yourself – it was not your fault. (Partner)

> Don't give up! Keep a high standard for yourself and be honest with your partner. Be accountable to someone else. Go all out to prove you can be trusted and if you fail – own up and don't give in. Don't let the shame consume you, acknowledge your mistakes and the guilt but don't let it destroy you. (Addicted partner)

> It's really hard and there are no magic answers or solution to getting through it, believe me, I wish there were! You have moments where you are literally on your knees because it's so hard to process and accept, but I also found there were moments that my husband and I were the closest we've ever been. There is no right or wrong way to react to it all or behave, but trust yourself and your emotions and go with them because they are all valid and need to be worked through. My main piece of advice I would give is you don't need all the details. At the time I wanted to know every last detail and despite two counsellors

telling me it was a really bad idea I went ahead and did it anyway. I trawled through emails and Facebook, trying to put names to faces, and compared myself to all of his affairs. I think I was trying to rationalise it and find some answers about his behaviour, but I have now come to the realisation that there are no answers or logical explanations, which is so frustrating and it took me a long time to accept that, but I think getting to that point is a real turning point in a partner's recovery. (Partner)

After 40+ years of lies (mainly through omission) and acting out the depth and breadth of partner pain is indescribable. Healing takes years not months. (Addicted partner)

Seek professional help, don't wait for this. (Partner and addicted partner)

Don't expect the fog in your partner's brain to be anything like clear. He will continue to lie to protect his addiction. After a lifetime of compulsive lying he will need to do a lot of work on the root causes of his addiction before he will start to face the pain and shame of the way he has lived his life. But if he keeps lying after this period, he's not in recovery and you will have some tough choices to make. For partners, whatever madness you are experiencing following discovery – it's normal. You are not unique, we've all gone through it and it's crap!! Read the literature, contact the support groups, get some specialist therapy, be careful what you say and who you tell, put your recovery needs before those of the addict. Be alive to the possibility that your addict will continue to try to gaslight and manipulate you during this period. (Partner)

Do not blame your partner and try to resist getting defensive and retaliating when your partner is angry/says hurtful things – it's not easy, but constantly bickering/arguing doesn't help. (Addicted partner)

Set boundaries, have an accountability contract, be gently assertive about what you need to feel safe. Then try to give him space. The more space I was able to give him, the closer we got and the more my husband started to see the light. (Partner)

References

Arterburn, S., Martinkus, J.B. (2014) *Worthy of Her Trust – What you need to do to rebuild sexual integrity and win her back*. Colorado Springs, CO: Waterbrook Press.

Baucom, D.H., Snyder, D.K., Gordon, K.C. (2011) *Helping Couples Get Past the Affair – A clinician's guide*. New York: The Guildford Press.

Stroebe, M., Schut, H. (1999) The dual process model of coping with bereavement: Rationale and description. *Death Studies*, *23*, 197–224.

Summary for couple therapists – the impact stage

The impact stage is the first stage couples struggling with sex addiction will need to go through. It is characterised by extreme displays of emotion, high levels of conflict and often trauma responses such as anxiety, depression, panic attacks and dissociation. The clinician's primary task is to ensure no further damage is done to the clients as individuals, or to the couple relationship. This usually requires slowing the process and holding firm therapeutic boundaries. During this phase therapy should focus on:

- Assessing for individual emotional safety, including suicide risk, PTSD and DVA (domestic violence/abuse) and sexual health
- Providing psycho-education on the impact stage
- Reducing conflict by establishing boundaries and improving communication skills
- Helping the couple to healthily manage extreme emotions
- Supporting the partner in their individual trauma recovery journey
- Supporting the addict in their individual addiction recovery journey
- Supporting the couple in developing an accountability contract and regularly checking that this is working for them
- Establishing a common understanding of sex or porn addiction
- Helping clients create an immediate accountability plan to help establish sobriety and stability

In addition to the above, couple therapists need to be aware of contracting issues around holding secrets and maintain vigilance to the possibility of getting caught in Malan's drama triangle. Further training in working with trauma and using multi-directional impartiality might also be required.

Part II

Assessing the damage

In Part II, the focus shifts to exploring the viability of the relationship. With both partners hopefully stronger as individuals, the task is to determine if the relationship can survive. The first chapter, Chapter 5, explains the importance of full disclosure in order to understand the extent of the damage caused. In Chapter 6 there are tools provided for each to assess the quality of their relationship, both before the discovery of sex or porn addiction, and now. With a greater understanding of the state of their relationship, Chapter 7 provides tools to allow couples to consider what the addiction means to them individually and as a couple, and includes practical tips and techniques for improving communication and mutual understanding. The final chapter in this section is where each can alone, and together, consider if they feel they want to save their boat and re-launch the relationship.

Chapter 5

Understanding the importance of disclosure

In Part II, our focus shifts to beginning to explore if the relationship can survive the tidal wave of addiction, or indeed, if both partners want it to survive. If both the person with the addiction is now active in recovery and the partner has built a greater sense of safety and personal stability, then it's time to look at the wreckage and see what can be salvaged. The first task in this process is disclosure, and this chapter will explain what disclosure is and why it's so important for both parties to move on, whether that's together or apart. This chapter will end with some thoughts and advice on telling others.

Before proceeding, it's important to say something about the timing of this chapter within this book. In Chapters 3 and 4 we explored why individual recovery needs to come first and how disclosure is most effective, and least damaging, if postponed to after the impact stage, but there are of course exceptions to this and times when an interim partial disclosure is important. The most common situation for this is when others know about acting out behaviours before a partner does, people who are not therapists or within the addicted partner's recovery community. For example, if any other close family member or friend knows, either through discovery, disclosure or revealed to by a third party, or if illegal activities have taken place and authorities are involved. As one partner shared in the survey for this book, "*I felt like the last to know and that brought up lots of feelings of humiliation and insecurities*". Partners have the right to know before anyone else outside of recovery, so if anyone else does know, or indeed, is likely to find out, then an earlier disclosure, at least of those particular behaviours, should be shared along the same guidelines as follow.

Most partners will have experienced at least some level of disclosure, or discovery, before and during the impact stage. Some may believe the disclosure is complete, others may suspect there is more to come. For the person with the addiction, some may know that their partner does not yet know everything, but be reluctant to share any more, while others may have already told everything, or at least everything they can remember or they believe to be 'relevant'. Either way, the process of disclosure is not complete until a formal disclosure has taken place, preferably within a therapeutic environment. The reasons for this are many, which we will look at in a while, but one of them is to attempt to repair damage caused in the first, earlier stages of disclosure or discovery.

As we saw in Chapter 1, there are four common ways that partners find out about the addiction, the sledgehammer blow, the drip, drip disclosure, the drip, drip exposure or the detective breakthrough. All of these carry trauma for the partner, shame for the addicted partner, and devastation for the couple relationship. The subsequent roller coaster of emotions that occur, often hallmarked by many hours of emotionally charged discussions and destructive arguments, can leave a legacy of pain within the relationship. Many partners are plagued with flashbacks to moments when more information was revealed, while the addicted partner may struggle to push these memories away out of shame. One key reason for a therapeutic disclosure is to reframe the experience into something that is safe and contained. Rather than reliving the tidal wave that shipwrecked the relationship and threw its members overboard, it takes place in the safety of a harbour where the facts can be seen from the perspective of having survived as individuals.

The therapeutic disclosure

The term 'therapeutic disclosure' is used to describe a process whereby the full history of acting out is told by the person with the addiction to the partner. It is a process of fact-finding and information-gathering. It is facilitated by a trained therapist whose job it is to ensure that the emotional and psychological needs of both are being cared for, both during and after the disclosure process. We will go on to look at the specifics of how this process unfolds in a moment, but first let's look at some more of the benefits of disclosure.

Benefits for the couple

- Draws a line under the information-seeking and -sharing process
- Allows both to remember and acknowledge what was shared during earlier, emotionally charged disclosures
- Provides a safe space to process any additional information that may be revealed
- Ensures an equal relationship, without secrets, where both parties know what happened
- Allows decisions to be made about the future based on truth
- Creates greater opportunities for intimacy to grow from shared knowledge of the past
- Provides information from which the accountability contract can be strengthened

Benefits for the partner

- Allows partners to stop seeking further information
- Provides greater understanding of past behaviours on which future decisions about the relationship can be made
- Creates a safe environment to explore other questions that need to be asked
- Provides information from which personal boundaries can be considered and established
- Minimises distractions from own personal recovery

Benefits for the addicted partner

- Draws a line under any further disclosures
- Provides the opportunity to break through secrecy and shame
- Removes the risk of any undisclosed information later being revealed or discovered
- Encourages honesty and vulnerability within the relationship
- If in 12-Step, provides space for Step 9 to be undertaken
- Allows the opportunity for true intimacy to develop, as they can be loved for who they really are, not who they're pretending to be.

For these benefits to be maximised, good timing is essential. A full disclosure is not advisable until some of the pain of initial disclosure has worn off and healthy coping strategies have been established for both. If there are significant additional secrets to be shared, then the disclosure process can be traumatic in itself, and could trigger further pain for the partner and relapse for the addicted partner. Therefore, it's essential that both partners have the psychological and emotional resources to manage it. This is another reason why it is important for the process to be conducted with a trained professional who can advise on appropriate timing and ensure that both partners are able to receive the ongoing support they need.

A therapeutic disclosure begins with a joint session where the couple are seen together to discuss the benefits, and risks, of a formal disclosure and explain the process and agree confidentiality boundaries. During this session, the timing of further sessions will be confirmed; it's always preferable to hold these sessions as closely together as possible, rather than extending over many weeks. Time can also be spent confirming that each has sufficient self-care in place after the disclosure session takes place and agree practical arrangements such as whether they will spend time apart afterwards and how children will be cared for if difficult emotions arise.

The couple session is followed by an individual session with the partner where they will be helped to list everything that is known and write a list of further questions that they may have – please do note the box 'What to disclose'. It is the therapist's job also to help a partner consider questions that they may not have previously thought of. The reason for this is that the goal is to draw a line under the disclosure process, which means doing everything possible to avoid a further question occurring in the future. Regrettably, this is not always possible, but common questions that partners may not have previously thought of, often because many assume the best, or are too traumatised to consider it, are questions like whether infidelity occurred during pregnancy or during a particularly difficult time in their family life, such as after a bereavement.

Once this list of facts and further questions is compiled, an individual session is offered to the addicted partner. During this session, a full history of acting out is taken and other questions presented as required. A therapist can often play a useful role in helping the addicted partner to remember anything that might previously been forgotten. Many people with addiction who have been acting out for many years will have forgotten some things – it's important to understand that this is not necessarily denial or avoidance, but simply the process of time and the fact that addiction takes place within a bubble that may have been compartmentalised. Asking supplementary questions to jog the memory can be helpful, for example, if trying to remember when a sex worker was first visited, a therapist may ask 'Where in the country did it occur?' 'Where you were working at the time?' 'How was the weather?' 'What car did you drive?' While these questions are in themselves irrelevant, they can help to take the person back in time and build a bigger picture.

Following this session, the addicted partner will write their disclosure letter (see example) ready for the next joint session, where it will be read to the partner. I always recommend the letter is shared with the therapist before the joint session to ensure all questions have been answered and there are no inadvertent, or deliberate, hints of minimisation or blame, such as 'I "only" visited two massage parlours' or 'I visited massage parlours while you were busy working away'. While both of these statements may be true, they can be triggering for a partner and it's a trigger that can be easily avoided. In addition to sharing information, it's important that the letter also demonstrates remorse and empathy for the partner rather than being a catalogue of facts. In this way, partners are able to hear that the addicted partner is taking full responsibility, not only for what's happened, but also for the hurt and pain they have caused their partners.

The next session with a therapist will be a joint one where the letter will be read by the addicted partner. I usually discuss with the couple how they would like this to be done, but generally advise that the addicted partner reads it in full to the partner first, then a copy is given to the partner to read through at their own pace and ask any further questions they may have for clarification. How a partner responds to a disclosure depends of course on what it contains and how much is new information. Another advantage of this happening with a therapist, one who has already seen the letter, is that hopefully they will be more prepared to help the couple process any traumatic response to further revelations.

While many therapeutic disclosures happen with one couple therapist, an increasingly common approach is for the partner and the addicted partner's individual therapists to collaborate together and manage the process between them. In this instance the joint sessions will happen with both therapists present and each individual therapist will take responsibility for preparing the question document with the partner and the disclosure letter with the addicted partner. This can be especially effective in giving both parties a sense of equality and fairness as both their needs are represented. Furthermore, it allows more space in individual therapy for the experience to be processed.

What to disclose

It is now recognised that receiving detailed, graphic information about acting out behaviours is not helpful to partners and is more likely to trigger a trauma response (Hall, 2016; Corley & Schneider, 2002; Corley et al., 2012). While many partners feel they are entitled to all the gory details, most regret it and realise later in their recovery that what they wanted was not necessarily what they needed. Regrettably, detailed information can build visual images in the brain which can be hard to get rid of, and while some partners may feel that this knowledge will be beneficial, evidence and experience shows that it's not. As a colleague reminds clients, this is a 'therapeutic' disclosure, not a 'forensic' disclosure. What a disclosure should include is:

- A broad outline of all acting out behaviours and timescales.
- A broad outline of places where acting out behaviours occurred – especially if they are places known to, or special to, a partner, including the family home.
- Any incidences of physical contact infidelity.
- Any incidences of emotional infidelity.
- Details of anyone known to the partner that was involved in acting out behaviours.
- Anything that may have put a partner at risk, such as health concerns, including STIs, financial and employment implications and any illegal activities.
- Any significant lies that have been told in the past to cover up behaviours.

A sample disclosure letter

Dear Sally,

This letter has taken me many hours to write and it has been one of the most painful experiences of my life. I am truly sorry for all the pain that I have caused you and I want you to know that I love you deeply and never wanted to hurt you. What follows is an account of all the ways in which I have betrayed you and put our relationship in jeopardy.

I first started viewing pornography when I was fourteen and I realise now that it had escalated out of control by the time I was in my second year of university – long before we met. I was also having sex with multiple partners, often compulsively but I didn't realise it at the time and justified to myself that it was what all young men did.

I thought all that was behind me when we met, but within the first year of our relationship I started watching pornography again. At first it was two or three times a week after you had gone to bed, but there were times when this was as much as five or six times. I used to lie to you that I was working, but I wasn't and sometimes I didn't come to bed until the early hours of the morning. I know that this affected our sex life and I was often not available for you in the way that you deserved.

I first had an affair when you were pregnant with Archie with someone at the office. I have never felt able to tell you this before because I know what an important time that was for us and I have tainted that time forever. It was one night when we were away at a conference and I felt huge guilt and shame. But it happened again six months later with the same person. After that I slept with three other women who I worked with before leaving that job.

When we moved to London I started visiting sex workers. Initially I went to massage parlours every other month, but this escalated to about twice a month over the following three years. At the parlours I received manual stimulation and on one occasion received oral sex. In 2011 I had sex with a prostitute for the first time and that was when I realised I had a significant problem. I had sex with two other prostitutes after that until you found out last August. Since then I have not had any kind of sexual encounter with anybody, but I continued viewing pornography compulsively on my work computer during office hours until March of this year. I can assure you that I have never looked at any illegal images on the computer and I always practiced safe sex to reduce the risk of you contracting a sexually transmitted infection. I have also never had sex with anyone you know or in any place that we have been to together, including our home. As far as I know, no one knows about my sexual acting out except for the people in my recovery group and the people we have told together.

Words cannot express how sorry I am for what I have done and how much shame and guilt I feel. I know I can't expect you to forgive me or expect you to want to stay with me. But I have never stopped loving you and I promise I will do everything in my power to stop this addiction and put you and our relationship first in my life.

John

Using a polygraph

Understandably, some partners are still left wondering if the formal disclosure process was complete and fully honest. After years of being deceived, lied to or gaslighted, the presence of a therapist, however well trained, does not in itself mean they will receive the full truth; as I know from experience, therapists can be lied to as well. The decision to use a polygraph, or lie detector, is a complex one as they too cannot be trusted to be fully accurate and tell the truth, but it's an option that many couples investigate. I am not an expert on polygraphs and the technology is rapidly changing, but it's important to understand that a polygraph will only give an indication of the likelihood that the truth is being told, not a categorical pass/fail answer. In my experience, agreeing in advance that a polygraph test will be undertaken after the disclosure to confirm that it was full and accurate is usually enough to ensure that it is. If an addicted partner refuses to take a polygraph test, then I suspect that tells you something in itself.

In the survey I asked what advice couples would give others about disclosure – here's what some of them said.

Disclosure is awful, but necessary and I think that's regardless of if you are moving on separately or trying to stay together.

I absolutely hated it and it's one of the most emotionally painful experiences of my life, but also a huge turning point in our recovery and relationship. (Partner)

I realised I couldn't live with the lies anymore. As horrible and painful as it is, it's an important part of the process. Make sure you disclose everything otherwise it makes it hard for your partner to trust you. (Addicted partner)

Disclosure for the addict is incredibly difficult. I just did not want anyone to know just how sordid and shameful my actions had been. I had to be dragged to disclosure and if truthful, I would have left a great deal undisclosed without my partner's tenacity in chasing the detail. The disclosure felt like we were going back into the abyss again, although we have progressed through it. (Addicted partner)

Think very carefully about the motives for disclosure and not disclosing – there are many pros and cons and it's not always easy to untangle emotional drivers like shame, fear, anxiety, anger, rage, etc. It can be difficult to be objective so guidance can be helpful. Also seek advice on what details are appropriate to share – do not 'buy' peace of mind at your partner's expense by unburdening your own shame and guilt. (Addicted partner)

Don't do disclosure like we did! We ripped each other apart. Very chaotic and unmanageable. Have a 'managed' therapeutic disclosure with therapists trained in such things. Accept that he may not remember all the dates and behaviours straightaway and that more may come out over time, which may not be a deliberate attempt to deceive, just that he's gained more clarity. (Partner)

The process of disclosure is one of the most widely written about in professional literature about sex addiction recovery (Schneider et al., 1998; Corley & Schneider, 2002; Steffens & Rennie, 2006; Schneider & Levinson, 2006; Corley et al., 2012; Carnes, 2018; Collins, 2018), but the one most often neglected by untrained professionals. If you're in couple counselling and your therapist hasn't talked to you about the benefits of having a therapeutic disclosure, ask why or find another therapist.

As we will explore later in Chapter 13, the essential ingredients for rebuilding trust are honesty, empathy and accountability – and until there has been a full disclosure, it's impossible for these to be fully activated. Making a full disclosure can feel frightening and risky, as it may rake up painful feelings in the past and reveal new ones. But it's a risk that's worth taking. Both partners and addicted partners can be very fearful of full disclosure, but research has shown that in spite of the pain and fears, both are glad that they did it (Schneider et al., 1998). Furthermore, in spite of over half of partners threatening to leave, less than a quarter actually did (Corley et al., 2012). For those who did leave, they left knowing exactly what they were walking away from and were better equipped to rebuild their lives.

After disclosure – what?

Undertaking a therapeutic disclosure is a major step and some partners find themselves feeling marooned afterwards. They now have all the facts they'd sought, all in one place, but the feelings haven't changed and they may have got worse, in part because there may have been further disclosures, but also because some of the old pain may have been dragged up again. Similarly, the addicted partner may feel marooned; they are free now of the burden of secrets, but shame may have increased with more revelations or with the sight of all their transgressions all exposed together in one place. They may also be struggling with a re-emergence of a partner's pain and feel that disclosure has made things worse, not better. Using our boat metaphor, the disclosure process is where you have both re-entered the wreckage, walked around and seen just how much damage has been done. It can feel overwhelming and the most important thing to do now is to recommit to self-care and your individual recovery as described in Chapter 3. Remember, the therapeutic disclosure is not necessarily about saving the relationship, it's about ensuring that both parties can clearly see the damage the tidal wave of addiction wreaked on their relation-ship. In the next chapter we will focus more closely on assessing the damage and in the next chapter we will explore how to construct meaning from the devastation, but first we'll talk about disclosure to others.

Telling others

In the last chapter we talked about the importance of protecting loved ones from the tidal wave and how some have regretted telling people too soon, but the decision about who to tell and what to tell is something that challenges most couples, especially those who have children. It's impossible to give categorical answers to the many questions that arise when thinking about disclosing to others, so I always advise talking through with a therapist or someone within your recovery or support community, but I hope that the following will also provide useful food for thought.

Think about each person you're thinking of disclosing to and consider the following.

- Is this coming from emotion, such as anger, guilt or shame? This is the most important thing to consider before telling anybody anything about what either of you is going through. If your motivation is coming from an emotion rather than from rational consideration, then you need to give yourself more time to think and seriously consider the following points. If you're not sure, then talk it through with someone you can trust to challenge you so you can be confident you're doing this for reasons you won't later regret.
- How will it benefit you? Consider if this person is someone who can provide valuable support for you either individually, or as a couple, or to your family, whether that's emotional or practical support.
- Will this person support you, whatever decision you make? Assuming you're reasonably confident this person can be a source of support, consider further if they'll continue to be a support to you, whatever decision you make in the future. In other words, will their support change if you later decide to end the relationship or stay in it?
- What impact is it likely to have on them? Finding out about sex or porn addiction can be a massive shock, as you both know from experience, and it will also be to others that you know. Some people can cope with this, others simply can't, and you may find yourselves having to support them, rather than being

able to turn to them for support. Therefore, you need to think carefully about the impact on them and whether they're resilient enough to hear what's happened. This is particularly true for children, elderly parents and those who are already experiencing struggles in their own lives.

- How much do you need to say? There will be some people that you want to tell everything to, such as a close friend or spiritual leader who can support you, but for others a partial disclosure may be safest for all. For example, you might tell close family members that the addicted partner has been unfaithful, but not say in what way, or that they're struggling with an addiction, but not say which one. Remember you can't unsay something, so always better to start cautiously and slowly disclose further information if and when it feels safe and appropriate.

- Do you need to tell them now? There may be people who you know you want to tell, but perhaps you don't need to tell them now. Many people will ask immediately if the relationship is going to continue; if you don't know, you may want to wait until you have a better idea, or are at least in the position of saying 'we're not sure but we'll be talking about this more in six months'. This is especially important for children of any age who will immediately worry about whether or not mum and dad are splitting up, and rather than risking giving assurances that you may renege on, it's often better to wait until a decision has been made and make do with partial disclosure in the meantime.

In all of this, remember there's a difference between privacy and secrecy. You're entitled to your own personal life, as individuals and as a couple. Remember also that people close to you who genuinely care about you will, and should, respect your privacy; hence, if you only tell them part of the story, or it's revealed over a period of time, they should be able to respect that. Others may be able to see that your relation-ship is going through a storm or even that it's battered and broken, but they don't have to know the reasons why. Ultimately you need to be guided by your motivation for telling others and ask 'is this a decision that I/we might later regret?' If the answer is yes, then now is not the time to disclose.

References

Carnes, S. (2018) Facilitated disclosure. In *The Routledge International Handbook of Sexual Addiction*, (edited by T. Birchard & J. Benfield), pp. 353–361. London: Routledge.

Collins, G. (2018) The process of couples therapy. In *The Routledge International Handbook of Sexual Addiction* (edited by T. Birchard & J. Benfield), pp. 212–223. London: Routledge.

Corley, M.D., Schneider, J.P. (2002). Disclosing secrets: guidelines for therapists working with sex addicts and co-addicts. *Sexual Addiction & Compulsivity*, 9(1): 43–67.

Corley, M.D., Schneider, J.P., Hook, J.N. (2012) Partner reactions to disclosure of relapse by self-identified sexual addicts. *Sexual Addiction and Compulsivity*, 19(4): 265–283.

Hall, P.A. (2016) *Sex Addiction – The Partner's Perspective*. London: Routledge.

Schneider, J.P., Corley, M.D., Irons, R.R. (1998) Surviving disclosure of infidelity: results of an international survey of 174 recovering sex addicts and partners. *Sexual Addiction and Compulsivity: The Journal of Treatment and Prevention*, 5: 189–217.

Schneider, J.P., Levinson, B. (2006) Ethical dilemmas related to disclosure issues: sex addiction therapists in the trenches. *Sexual Addiction and Compulsivity*, 13(1): 1–39.

Steffens, B.A., Rennie, R.L. (2006) The traumatic nature of disclosure for wives of sexual addicts. *Sexual Addiction & Compulsivity*, 13(2–3): 247–267.

Chapter 6

Analysing the condition of your relationship

So now the truth, the whole truth, and nothing but the truth is out there and known by both of you – or at least, that is what I hope. Regrettably, that is not always the outcome of a therapeutic disclosure, occasionally other details are disclosed or discovered, but if you've gone through the process fully, you should both have a shared understanding of the damage caused by the tidal wave. Now the impact stage is over and you have each started work on your own recovery, you should both also be in a stronger place to look objectively at your relationship and begin to analyse what's left of your relation-ship. This will give you the vital information you need to start the decision-making process of whether there is anything worth salvaging.

How damaged your relation-ship is will depend on two factors. First, the size of the tidal wave, which hopefully you are both now fully aware of post-disclosure, and second, how strong your relationship was before the tidal wave hit. The relationships that survive the devastation of sex addiction are those that were built solidly in the first place. You may have a massive hole in the hull, but if other areas are still largely intact, then you may be able to set sail again – if you wish.

This chapter provides an assessment tool that you can undertake alone and then share together to help you consider the condition of your relationship, and the areas where you would like to see change and growth. Please understand, this is not to suggest that the state of your relationship was in any way the 'cause' of the addiction – that was purely the responsibility of the addicted partner – but rather assessing how you each feel about your relationship will help you consider what you want to do about it. We will start with a general question about perceived relationship satisfaction and then explain the different components of a relationship and why each is important to relationship satisfaction. Let me stress again, it's important that both of you have undertaken some of your own recovery work before undertaking these exercises. It is not possible to objectively analyse anything while in the grip of addiction or in the wake of trauma. Both of you need to be standing on solid ground – still shaking, perhaps, but at least knowing that you are safe and can survive.

General relationship satisfaction

In the survey I undertook for this book, I asked couples to rate their relationship satisfaction between 0 and 10 before the tidal wave hit, and now (we'll read more about the 'now' responses in Part IV). All of the couples were 18 months post-disclosure when they completed the questionnaire and all but one described their general satisfaction in the relationship above 5. What becomes quickly apparent as you read their comments is that, with hindsight, they are each able to see that their relationship was not as good as they thought. Some are able to attribute the difficulties directly to the addiction, while others recognise that there were other influences and contributory factors. Here's what some of them said:

> I couldn't bear to be around my wife, or even at home. Partly because of the shame and guilt but also because I'd separated myself from my family through my actions. (Addicted partner – rated 2)

> I genuinely didn't think it was bad. We have always got on really well and spent lots of time together. There were times when my husband would seem a bit distant (I now know why) but the majority of the time I would have said we had a good relationship. (Partner – rated 7)

> In many areas of our relationship I felt that everything was perfect, I realise now that it wasn't, but at the time I was happy in our relationship ... My partner worked away ... we moved house ... I see now I was extremely resentful and it was having a big impact on me. (Addicted partner – rated 8)

> I was happily married and expected to remain so until death did us part. (Partner – rated 9)

> I felt we'd got on well together ... I don't think either of us realised how dysfunctional our relationship had been in various areas – both had considerable baggage from the past. (Addicted partner – rated 8)

> I called my husband my 'rock' ... I filtered out all of the crap ... I made lots of compromises. I didn't know how to do healthy relationships. (Partner – rated 7)

Hindsight is both a gift and a curse as it provides us with the ability to see our past in a different light and through a different lens, which inevitably alters our perception of the reality we experienced. Nonetheless, if you have never experienced your relationship as satisfying, then it may be difficult to find anything on which to rebuild. Whereas, if you can attribute most of the difficulties you experienced to the addiction, then once in recovery, many of those difficulties will dissipate. If you're not sure which of the difficulties are due to the addiction and which stem from other issues you may have had in your past, or from life circumstances, the following will help you. You may also find it helpful to talk through with your counsellor.

Assessing your relationship

Couple relationships are complicated. Unlike any other kind of relationship, you live together and share almost every aspect of your life together, including parenting, finances, running a home, supporting other family members, spending time with friends, relaxing and most likely, sharing a sexual relationship. There are so many things that a couple has to collaborate on, and compromise with, in order to achieve a satisfying relationship. There are four broad components to every couple relationship, and we will look at each of these in turn.

Compatibility

Compatibility is one of the most important components of a satisfying relationship, sharing common interests and the same outlook on life and goals for the future, but it's also something that is not always easy to identify. It is too simplistic to say 'yes' or 'no' when considering whether you're compatible; rather, understand that it is a continuum, with 'very similar' at one end, and 'completely different' at the other. Furthermore, there are many different areas of compatibility and as people change and grow over the years, they become more or less compatible in some of those areas.

Research has shown that it is how we perceive those differences between us that ultimately make the difference between whether or not we are happy within a relationship (Zentner, 2005). For example, if it's essential to you that someone shares your passion for golf or politics, then scoring high in compatibility will matter to you, while for someone else, that may not be important. There are no hard and fast rules on how compatible we need to be. Some couples thrive on difference and that's what keeps their relationship interesting and evolving, while for others, those same differences feel like wedges that drive them apart. For most people, our ability to manage those differences will come from our own family and relationship history, as well as our personality. More importantly, our ability to negotiate and compromise when couple differences collide is based on our ability to communicate (more on this later). However, there are some areas where compatibility is important and where compromise may involve too high a degree of personal sacrifice: where compromise touches the deepest part of who we are, the aspects of ourselves we fundamentally don't ever want to change. The two areas where most of us do not want to compromise are our values and our personal goals in life.

Our values form the bedrock of our personality and define what gives our lives a sense of meaning and purpose. When couples don't share the same value system, then they inevitably become acrimonious or fail. Addiction robs people of their values as they increasingly manipulate, lie, deceive and betray to fuel their addictive needs. Similarly, the trauma of betrayal often leaves partners breaking their own value system, as they often also find themselves lying and manipulating to get the truth, or becoming abusive and aggressive through rage. Regrettably, to a lesser or greater degree, we all behave outside of our value system at some stage in our lives, but nonetheless, our values don't change. We believe in them, even if we don't live by them. But if couples don't share the same values, such as honesty, fidelity, empathy, fairness, compassion; and if these aren't put into practice in similar ways, such as respect for self, caring for family, tolerance of others and financial transparency, then your differences may be too far apart.

Our goals in life often stem from our values and hence if you don't share the same fundamental values, you may not agree on the type of future you want to share and failing to reach those life goals may leave you feeling deeply dissatisfied with life. If one of you is committed to having children and the other isn't, or if one of you wants to sell up and retire at 50 to travel the world while the other wants to invest in building a bigger home, or if one of you wants to follow a particular faith tradition together or join a swinging community and the other doesn't, then even if you are able to rebuild your relation-ship, you'll never be happy sailing in the same direction together.

Intimacy

Intimacy is a difficult thing to accurately define, but most people understand it as feeling close and connected to their partner. It's been suggested that one of the reasons many couples struggle with intimacy is because they define it too narrowly or rely on only one type of intimacy to sustain their relationship, such as sexual intimacy (Fife, 2017). Intimacy and intensity are often confused by someone with an addiction (Weiss, 2015) and while there's no doubt that a shared intense experience will provide a level of connectedness, intimacy is also found in the quieter, more gentle experience of knowing someone and sharing a life with them over many, many years. In Esther Perel's excellent book, *Mating in Captivity* (Perel, 2007), she shares how 'talk intimacy' has taken over from so many other ways that people can express intimacy. We all communicate, all of the time, and we don't always have to use words. We communicate with touch, a smile, a wink, through collaboration on tasks, with gestures of kindness and thoughtfulness. When we rely on speech as the only way to connect, we may run the risk of confusing intimacy with intrusion.

Some think the opposite of intimacy is distance, but it's also autonomy. All of us need private space and have a right to maintain our own private thoughts and feelings. We will talk about this much further in Part III, but for now, let's look at some of the key areas of intimacy:

- *Emotional* – being similar in your emotional expression, whether that's getting angry or sad by the same things or being equally robust or sensitive.
- *Intellectual* – being on the same wavelength, sharing thoughts and ideas, being able to understand each other's thought processes.
- *Physical* – enjoying sharing affection through touch, sensuality and sexuality as well as being in tune with each other's physical demonstration of emotion.
- *Recreational* – being able to spend time together laughing, relaxing and having fun, whether that's as a couple, a family or with friends.
- *Spiritual* – whether it's religion, politics, the environment or a love of animals, being able to share these passions with similar levels of fervour, or indeed, the same lack of it.

As you read through this list you may have instantly recognised areas where you would like to feel more connected; perhaps you've never been close in these areas, or the addiction has got in the way. Or it may be that your lifestyle has got in the way, which we will look at now.

Lifestyle

Many couples fall out about the practical day-to-day living arrangements of their life and over issues that affect the lifestyle they want to lead. While some issues are relatively trivial, others are important and they often cause considerable frustration, resentment and acrimony. Some couples manage their lives together harmoniously, whether that's running a home, caring for family or managing finances, whereas for others, the effort of constant negotiations over practicalities leaves them feeling exhausted and drained, with little energy to enjoy other aspects of the relationship. Below is a list of common lifestyle issues that can cause difficulties, and at the end of the chapter you'll find the assessment tool where you can indicate how satisfied you were in each of these areas of the relationship before the tidal wave hit.

- *Home* – who should do what and how it should be done, including housework, laundry, cooking, shopping, paying the bills, decorating and fixing the boiler.
- *Parenting* – like home, who should do what and how it should be done, including what food the children should eat, what time they should go to bed, what discipline is appropriate and how sparingly it should be used. Also how involved each of you should be as parents in terms of providing emotional, practical and financial support.
- *Friends* – how often is it acceptable to see your individual friends and when should you see friends as a couple. How much is appropriate to share with friends and how much influence they should have on your lives.
- *Hobbies and pastimes* – whether you should do things together or apart and how much of a priority leisure should be in your lives, including less leisurely activities such as health and fitness.
- *In-laws* – for some couples, extended family is a particularly emotive issue and if they've been a contributory factor in the addiction, or there has been a fall-out since disclosure, it can be particularly sensitive. If you've always disagreed on how involved they should be in your lives, then this may become more difficult now.
- *Money* – another highly emotive topic for some couples. How much should you spend, on what and whom and how much should you save and what should you save it for?
- *Work* – how much of a priority should work be and how much will you let it influence your home life, whether that's long hours, technology use at home, business travel, or moving home; can you agree on what a healthy work–life balance looks like?

The decisions we make about the way we run our lives often feel like imperatives and that's why the list above includes so many 'shoulds', and why lifestyle issues can cause so much conflict between couples. In reality, there are many right ways to parent, manage your finances, deal with in-laws and balance work and leisure, and only a few wrong ways. How you have managed your differences in the past will largely depend on your ability to effectively communicate with each other.

Communication

If we follow the metaphor of your relationship being like a boat, communication is the rudder. Without good communication it will always be difficult to steer in the direction you both want to go and you'll often find yourselves running aground or drifting aimlessly. Good communication means being able to speak in a way that can be heard and listen in a way that demonstrates that you've understood. We'll look at this in more depth in our next chapter, but as couples we need effective communication skills for sharing essential information, passing the time of day, sharing personal thoughts and feelings, building intimacy and resolving differences. When we think about good communication, we tend to only think of the deeper kinds of conversations we have or how we do or don't resolve conflict, but for a satisfying relationship, the following five types of communication are required.

- *Information updates* – the type of information you need to share with each other to keep your home and lifestyle running smoothly, for example what time you'll be home, whether you've run out of milk, if the car needs to be booked in for an MOT or a child taken to the dentist.
- *Small talk* – the general chit chat about what you've done today, what you'd like to do at the weekend, how the weather is and the news headlines.
- *Companionable chat* – this kind of conversation goes beyond small talk and is about sharing more about your personal thoughts and feelings about yourself and your life.
- *Intimate sharing* – this is where you are able to talk on a deeply personal level, sharing difficult emotions and being vulnerable with each, while trusting the other person will handle what they hear with care and respect.
- *Conflict resolution* – as we've seen, all couples will have differences of opinion, some minor, some major, and the ability to work through these differences in a healthy way is essential, especially in the aftermath of sex and porn addiction.

We will talk further about communication in Chapter 7 and in Part IV, but if you know that this is an area where you need to develop your relationship, whether that's as a couple or as separated parents who still need to talk about the children, then seeking couple counselling will be beneficial and you'll also find further recommended reading at the end of this book.

The Relationship Assessment Tool

Below you will find a summary of all the components of a relationship that we've been looking at in this chapter. Take some time to look through and tick the box that most represents how you felt, 'before' the addiction became known to you both. If you're the partner, I fully appreciate that this will be a difficult exercise, as finding out about the addiction will understandably have left you doubting what you thought you knew about your past. Nonetheless, your reality, as you experienced it then, is still important and this exercise will help you to see more clearly what needs to change if you stay and what you'll lose if you leave. Please be reassured, again, that this exercise in no way indicates that you are to blame in any way for the addiction.

It's best to do this exercise individually and then share with each other once completed. If you fear that this will create more conflict or upset for either of you, then consider sharing the results within a couple counselling session.

Before disclosure, how satisfied were you with each of the following areas of your relationship?	Very satisfied	Reasonably satisfied	Often dissatisfied	Very dissatisfied
Compatibility				
Values				
Life goals				
Intimacy				
Emotional				
Intellectual				
Physical				
Recreational				
Spiritual				

Before disclosure, how satisfied were you with each of the following areas of your relationship?	Very satisfied	Reasonably satisfied	Often dissatisfied	Very dissatisfied
Lifestyle				
Home				
Parenting				
Friends				
Hobbies and pastimes				
In-laws				
Money				
Work				
Communication				
Information updates				
Small talk				
Companionable chat				
Intimate sharing				
Conflict resolution				

Hopefully you both have a better awareness of the condition of your relationship before the tidal wave struck. Having this information to hand will help you in the next chapter, where we look at how you begin to make the decision about whether to separate or work at rebuilding your relationship. But before we move onto that, we will look at five essential ground rules for any successful relationship.

Ground rules of a successful relationship

For a couple relationship to be happy and fulfilling for both, it needs to be built on a firm foundation where each partner understands, believes and commits to the same ground rules. These ground rules will help you not only build a healthy relationship, but to maintain it, whatever the future might bring. If your relationship already has these ground rules in place, then you'll be in a stronger position to move on together if you choose, but if some are missing, or have been damaged by the addiction, then you'll need to work on these before addressing the issues you've identified through the relationship assessment. Take some time to read through the below and consider how you would mark yourself on a score of 0–10 on each ground rule. I recommend you do this alone, or within individual therapy, before sharing with your partner.

- *Love yourself* – low self-esteem wrecks relationships because it makes you dependent on your partner for your well-being and ultimately, if you can't love yourself, it's hard to believe that someone else will. Addiction and betrayal trauma wreck self-esteem, at least in the short term, and whether your relationship survives or not, it's your responsibility to put it back together again. Furthermore, if you want to work at rebuilding your relationship, you have a responsibility to your partner, as well as yourself, to learn how to love yourself, whatever your faults and failings. For addicted partners, humility is often confused with low self-esteem and their guilt and shame may keep them trapped in self-loathing, but if you don't rebuild your self-worth, you will become unhealthily reliant on your partner's approval and be more vulnerable to relapse. For partners, rebuilding self-esteem is not only important for their own mental health, but also for minimising triggers and rebuilding trust, as it builds resilience and a boundary between what the addicted partner does and the damage they are able to cause. Hopefully if you are at least six months post-disclosure and have started your individual recovery journeys, then you will already be working on any self-esteem issues, but if there's more work to do, then continue doing it.

On a scale of 0–10, where 0 is 'not at all' and 10 is 'completely', where would you mark yourself? _____
- *Like your partner* – love is an emotion, and like all emotions, it is never constant, but fluctuates along with mood and circumstances. A successful relationship is not like a Hollywood movie or epitomised by an annual Valentine's card, and many a relationship is damaged by unrealistic expectations of constant romance and unconditional love. As Russell Grieger advises in *The Couples Therapy Companion* (Grieger, 2013, p. 7), "there is no such thing as unconditional love, except perhaps for children and pets. Love dies if it's not nourished". Modern notions of

romantic love have damaged many relationships because when someone doesn't 'feel' in love, they're tempted to stop doing the work of 'loving'. Love is a verb, it's something you do, not something you feel. It's a commitment to continue to treat someone with care and respect, regardless of how you feel. As we said in the first chapter of this book, addiction robs both the partner and the addicted partner of their experience of love and will leave both doubting if it was ever there, but one question you can hopefully ask yourself is 'do I like my partner?' Like may seem like a feeble word in comparison to love, but it's the closest we have in English to the word *philia*, which is Greek for affectionate love. If you are able to like your partner, in spite of what you've gone through, and you continue to care about them, even if at times you hate them, then this is a solid foundation on which to rebuild.

On a scale of 0–10, where 0 is 'not at all' and 10 is 'completely', where would you mark yourself? _____

• *Accept your differences* – with the exception to the importance of sharing core values and life goals, a successful relationship accepts that there may be significant differences between you. We are all unique human beings, which means we think differently, have different emotions, handle those emotions differently, do things differently, have different tastes, have different opinions, and so on and so on. Those differences mean there will inevitably be times when you don't understand each other and many couples waste years of their life trying to 'understand' rather than simply 'accept'. Couples coming to terms with sex addiction are bombarded by differences between them that they never knew existed. Partners are traumatised by those differences, seeing a side of their addicted partner that they never thought existed, and addicted partners are often surprised by their partner's reactions. If you feel your relationship can't be rebuilt until you see the world through the same eyes, or until you 'understand' your differences, then you'll have a very long wait. But when you learn to accept differences as a part of our humanity, without judgement or fear, then we have the chance to learn from them and through curiosity, become closer.

On a scale of 0–10, where 0 is 'not at all' and 10 is 'completely', where would you mark yourself? _____

- *Adapt to change* – to survive in the world, and certainly within relationships, we all need to be willing to adapt to change. We often confuse certainty with stability and live our lives with the illusion that we are in control of our lives and we only struggle when things change. But in reality, life is constantly changing and will always be unpredictable. Those changes come from both internal and external factors and they change us as individuals and also as partners within a relationship. Recovery from addiction requires significant internal change for the addicted partner and for their partner. It involves many lifestyle changes for the addict, which in turn, inevitably affects the partner's lifestyle choice. If you want to rebuild your relationship you'll have to be able to adapt to change. All relationships, and people, change, from internal and external life factors and life stages. Whether we survive as individuals and as couples depends on our capacity to adapt to those changes. Recovery will bring significant change, as will surviving the trauma. Neither of you will be the same and that's the first change you'll need to adapt to. But as you continue to go through different life stages together, there will be other challenges and changes too. Are you willing to adapt?

On a scale of 0–10, where 0 is 'not at all' and 10 is 'completely', where would you mark yourself? _____

- *Communicate* – communication is the bridge across difference and the road to intimacy; without it, you won't survive. Even if you stay together, you'll feel lonely and isolated from each other. You need to be willing to talk more and listen more than you talk. If communication is one-way, or if you're not willing to talk anymore or listen any harder, then it's already the end of the road. Healthy communication means learning to talk, even when you don't think you've got anything to say, and learning to listen, even when what you hear may be uncomfortable or feel unimportant.

On a scale of 0–10, where 0 is 'not at all' and 10 is 'completely', where would you mark yourself? _____

In completing this exercise you may recognise areas where you may need to make personal changes as well as changes as a couple. You may never get to the stage where you can rate yourself at 10 in all areas, and there may be days when you feel very differently, but if you both accept that these ground rules are important, and you're both willing to commit to them, then that's an excellent start.

Now you've completed the exercises in this chapter you will be in a much stronger position to know what is left of your relation-ship. Which elements are intact and which would need either rebuilding, or building from scratch. You will also understand the essential ground rules for beginning to rebuild, if you both choose to do so.

References

Fife, S.T. (2017) *Aspects of Intimacy, Techniques for the Couple Therapist – Essential interventions from the experts*, Chapter 30, pp. 145–150. London: Routledge.

Grieger, R. (2013) *The Couples Therapy Companion – A cognitive behavior workbook*. Hove: Routledge.

Perel, E. (2007) *Mating in Captivity*. London: Hodder & Stoughton.

Weiss, R. (2015). *Sex Addiction 101: A basic guide to healing from sex, porn and love addiction*. Deerfield Beach, FL: Health Communications.

Zentner, M.R. (2005) Mate personality concepts and compatibility in close relationships: A longitudinal analysis. *Journal of Personality and Social Psychology*, 89(2): 242–256.

Chapter 7

Navigating the meaning stage

In the last chapter we explored what was left of your relation-ship after the tidal wave of addiction had struck. We looked at whether any of the core structures were still in one piece and which areas were already weak and in need of repair before the storm hit. Our focus now moves to gaining a better mutual understanding of what has happened to your relationship. You are hopefully now at the stage in your journey where you have far more knowledge about the tidal wave that hit your relation-ship, but like many couples, you may still be struggling to know what this means. Your feet are back on dry land, though undoubtedly you'll still be feeling rather seasick, and you have a better sense of what's left of your relation-ship and per-haps a greater awareness of just how much needs to be rebuilt if it's ever going to float again. In this we will look at the three tasks of constructing meaning, namely sharing how you feel, sharing what you've learned and sharing what you need. Exercises are provided to help each of you make sense of the damage caused and share that information with each other in a way that can help you to restore a sense of sanity and stability and not cause further harm to your relationship.

Constructing meaning is the second stage of recovery for couples recovering from the trauma of infidelity (Baucom et al., 2011). It means developing a shared, coherent understanding of why the addiction occurred, one that can replace earlier explanations of the impact stage where denial and blame is rife. Once a mutual understanding has been reached, it is much easier for couples to have compassion with themselves as well as with each other and to feel and demonstrate empathy. If the relationship is to survive, this is essential, but even if it doesn't, this richer and deeper understanding allows couples to separate and move on with their lives, letting go of the confusion and resentments that can plague self-esteem and sabotage future relationships. The process of constructing meaning can be a truly cathartic process, but regrettably also a painful one. It can also present a significant challenge to communication as many couples find themselves viewing their relation-ship from very different perspectives. If you're the person with the addiction, like many, you may be feeling impatient to start the rebuild and set sail again; and if you're the partner, you may be staggered that your spouse seems to have so little understanding of how you're feeling and where you are. You may both be on dry land, but it may feel like you've swum to different continents. The exercises here will help you to express how you each feel, and hear the other's perspective. We will first look at some communication strategies that will help you to navigate this journey as smoothly as possible.

Constructive communication

Constructive communication is the backbone of any happy relation-ship. As well as making life easier on a day-to-day basis, good communication also allows couples to be comfortable with differences and deepen intimacy. Constructive communication skills allow us to share our thoughts and feelings with our partners and know they'll be heard, and they help us demonstrate that we're open to hearing their thoughts and feelings, and these dialogues enable us to enter into each other's worlds and see life through each other's eyes. As we do this, we grow in understanding of one another and relationships improve.

How you communicate with your partner today is based on what you've learnt and the skills you've developed over your lifetime. Over the years you're likely to pick up some good habits but also some bad ones, but you may not always know which ones are which! Our communication style is also influenced by our culture and our values. For example, some people are brought up in families where it's encouraged to openly share whatever you think and feel, whereas in other families the message is not to say anything that might potentially hurt or embarrass someone else. Both families would probably say they uphold the values of honesty, openness, kindness and consideration, but when it comes to communication style, they prioritise some over others. Previous relationships also play a role. You may have had your fingers burned in the past and learned that it was better to stay quiet, or you may have been criticised for not sharing your feelings enough. Whatever you've learned in the past, what matters now is developing a communication style with each other that allows both of you to speak and be heard. What follows now are some guidelines for developing more constructive communication.

Communication guidelines

- *Agree an objective* – if either of you wants to talk, first agree what the conversation is going to be about. Do you want to resolve a particular issue? Make a complaint? Share your feelings? Have a two-way discussion on a topic? Share one of the following exercises? Or perhaps – just have a rant? If it's the latter, that's OK, but it will be easier for both of you if the objective is clear from the outset.
- *Check your motivation* – similar to the above, but this is a reality check for each of you. Are you sure you're having this conversation now because it's important to you? Would you be talking to someone else who will be able to advise, or empathise with you better, such as a therapist or someone in your recovery or support group? Is something else going on that might be influencing how you're feeling? Are you ready to be fully open with your own thoughts and feelings? Are you willing to listen, even if what you hear is a very different perspective to your own? Are you able to remain open-minded?
- *Choose your timing* – the right environment is crucial to a constructive conversation. You should do all you can to ensure you won't be interrupted and be confident there's enough time for the conversation; in other words, not five minutes before one of you has to leave the house. If possible, avoid a time when either of you may be particularly stressed or hormonal and always avoid times when alcohol is involved or late at night. If you want to be heard, then you both have to take responsibility for choosing a time when that's more likely to be the case.

- *Stick to the subject* – when emotions run high it's easy to get knocked off topic, to rake up the past and drag in other people's opinions to back up your own, or simply to get distracted and move on to something that's not relevant right now. If you've agreed an objective, try to stick to it.
- *Start sentences with I* – this is a very simple rule that can be very effective. When we start sentences by saying 'I think ...', 'I feel ...' it is much easier to listen to and less provocative than 'you made me feel ...' or 'you think ...'. Take responsibility and own what you're thinking and feeling. You don't have to justify it, just own it.
- *No absolutes* – using absolutes often escalates a conversation into an argument. Using words that are broad generalisations are rarely true and generally provoke a defensive reaction. For example, saying 'everyone thinks ...' or 'you always do ...' or 'you never ...'. Never say *never* or *always* or *should* or *shouldn't*.
- *Express your thoughts and feelings* – often we feel misunderstood because we share only our thoughts or only our feelings. For example, we may say 'I feel hurt and angry when you're late from work', but with nothing else added a partner may wonder why, or make a wrong assumption. Whereas if we say 'I feel angry when you're late because I think I'm not as important as your job' it can begin to make sense. Or if we share just a thought, 'I think I'm not as important as your job', without saying 'and consequently I feel hurt and rejected', a partner may be left without any comprehension of the impact their lateness has.
- *Listen attentively and respectfully* – we talk about the importance of being a good listener so often, but few of us make sufficient effort to demonstrate we really are listening. First and foremost, you need to give your partner your full attention, no checking mobiles, or flicking the remote control, or any other distraction. Ensuring you're facing your partner and giving regular eye contact is important, as is restating what you've heard, summarising key points, asking for clarification if necessary and allowing space to finish their train of thought. We all construct sentences at different speeds and demonstrating impatience is a sure-fire way of showing you're not listening respectfully, as is saying 'you've said this before'. If your partner is telling you again, then

it's because 'you' didn't demonstrate that you were listening the first time.

- *Show empathy* – showing empathy is another essential element of listening, and we will talk about empathy much more in Chapter 13. But in brief, what it means in communication is demonstrating that you understand the emotional message, as well as the factual one. This can be done by mirroring body language, repeating back the emotions stated and sharing that you know how that emotion feels.

- *Stay calm or use time out* – this is perhaps an obvious one, but if you're trying to have a constructive conversation, rather than just air angry feelings, try to keep emotions in check when possible. That doesn't mean you can't become tearful or show some irritation, but if you're beginning to feel overwhelmed by emotion it's either time for a time out (see Chapter 4), or change the objective of the conversation and admit that you now just need to show how you're feeling and go back to the original conversation another day.

Before we end this section on constructive communication, it's important to recognise how each of us can have our own subtle ways of sabotaging a conversation when it's one we don't really want to have or makes us feel uncomfortable. The most common ones include expecting mind-reading, or thinking you're a mind-reader. In other words, thinking your partner should know how you think and feel or assuming you know this about them. Going into a monologue is another way of subtly stopping someone having their say or the opposite, being silent or constantly interrupting until they give up or get angry. The one that I hear most often in my counselling room when working with couples and sex addiction is what has become known as dropping the 'D' bomb – in other words, knocking a difficult conversation off track by going straight to talking about divorce or separation. While it's true that there will inevitably be times when trying to communicate is futile, the 'D' bomb is probably the fastest way of stopping almost any conversation from being constructive.

These guidelines can help you in every area of your communication, not just with each other but also with others close to you.

It's not always easy to stick to them, but if you can both commit to trying to, and give each other the benefit of the doubt when you fail, then you will both benefit from reduced conflict and feeling misunderstood and unheard. We will now move on to the three tasks of the meaning stage with the hope that these guidelines will have equipped you to work through them.

Task one – sharing how you are

This task should be undertaken *after* you've had a therapeutic disclosure. It's an opportunity, particularly for partners, to share the impact that the disclosure has had on them. Ideally there should be some space for reflection before this is undertaken and emotions have stabilised, and is often best undertaken within a safe and holding therapeutic relationship. It takes the form of writing letters, which are then read out to each other, but if you prefer to be less formal and make notes for yourself to then share with your partner, then that is obviously fine. The advantage of writing it as a letter for yourself first is that it gives you time to process before sharing, but it really depends on how you're feeling emotionally and how constructive the communication is between you. It is perhaps easiest to read on and then discuss as a couple before deciding the practicalities of how you will share how you are, but either way, it's important that the partner shares first.

The emotional impact letter (partner)

Some partners find this an incredibly powerful exercise, while for others it can reopen wounds that have already begun to close. It is most beneficial for partners who feel as though they have not had the opportunity to fully express how they feel or for those who feel they have repeatedly tried to share it, but it has not been heard.

Writing an impact letter is the place where a partner can write openly and honestly about how they feel; the impact the deception, infidelity and process of disclosure has had on their lives. It may include some practical information, such as struggling at work or turning down a promotion opportunity because of stress, or missing out on family occasions, but primarily it's about sharing the emotional impact. It can be helpful to consider this impact mentally and emotionally, in other words, how it has affected how you think and feel in the following areas: how you think and feel about yourself, your partner, the relationship, your family, your friends, your work, your lifestyle, the world in general, and finally your future. Simply writing it all down in one place can be therapeutic, but it can also feel overwhelming, hence why I recommend this is done within a therapeutic and supportive environment.

It's important when writing the letter to stay focused on your own thoughts and feelings, without blame or judgement. That's often easier said than done, especially if anger is still running high, but the objective is to state the impact as the consequence of the addiction, not to feel any need to justify why you feel it or where it came from. When shared, the hope is that it will be met with empathy, rather than defensiveness or self-focused shame, hence saying 'I feel unable to trust or feel close to any of my male friends' is better than 'you have made it impossible for me to trust or feel close to any of my friends'.

Writing an impact letter usually takes time and can be lengthy; when worked through in individual therapy, you can be helped to consider each area in turn where your life has been impacted. Once complete, the letter can then be shared in a joint session, and like the therapeutic disclosure session, this should be managed and contained and the needs of both parties should be considered before, during and after the process.

The emotional restitution letter (addicted partner)

Hearing a partner's impact letter is perhaps one of the toughest experiences someone with an addiction is going to go through. If you're in a 12-Step fellowship and have already worked through Steps 1–8, you will at least be ready in part, but nonetheless, seeing the pain all in one place is hard. The emotional restitution letter is a response to the impact letter, but it can be used independently as part of Step 9, making amends, and worked through either with a sponsor and/ or a therapist. The objective of the restitution letter is threefold: to validate the partner's feelings, to express empathy and to own your own behaviours. We will look at each of these in turn.

- *Validate feelings* – partners need to know that their feelings have been heard and valued. That means acknowledging those feelings as being appropriate and understandable. To do this you need to focus specifically on what has been said and illustrate that you understand why your behaviours – the acting out behaviours, the deceit and your reactions since disclosure – have created or exacerbated those feelings. For example, in response to the example in the impact letter you might say 'I understand that you feel unable to trust your male friends because I broke your trust and I am the one who you should feel able to trust the most'. Validating feelings is a cognitive process of demonstrating rational understanding of someone's emotions, but this in itself is not enough: you also need to show that you can connect emotionally with those feelings.
- *Express empathy* – empathy is about feeling the feelings of another; being willing, and able, to put yourself in their shoes, viewing the situation from their perspective and feeling their pain. Empathy is a painful experience because it means climbing down into the pit of despair and staying there long enough to know what it feels like.
- *Own your behaviours* – when writing a restitution letter, it's important to make it clear that you are taking full responsibility for your acting out behaviours, the decision to lie and deceive and anything hurtful or thoughtless that you've done or said since disclosure or discovery. No blame, no defensiveness, no minimisation or excuses.

It's important to recognise that the restitution letter is not a letter of apology, although that doesn't mean that you can't say sorry or demonstrate remorse, but rather a place to put in writing that you have 'heard' your partner and understand the mental and emotional impact the addiction has had on them. This is also your opportunity to share how you feel about what you've done. Like the therapeutic disclosure and the impact letter, it's best to share your restitution letter within a safe therapeutic environment and ensure you both have ongoing support afterwards.

In this exercise, you will both have the opportunity to share with each other what you have learned on your individual recovery journey – so far. Like task one, you may find this easier to undertake within therapy or with someone else in recovery, and you may want to take time to write it so you have time to reflect, before sharing with your partner. For the person with the addiction, this involves explaining why you became addicted, the behaviours you engaged in that ensured your partner didn't know the truth and your recovery plan moving forward. For the partner, it means sharing what you've learned about the ways you consciously or unconsciously contributed to the maintenance of the addiction, and the ways your behaviours may have hindered you finding the truth sooner. In this task it is the addicted partner's turn to share first and the partner to respond.

This can be a difficult process for both, but as Collins and Collins explain in their book, *A Couples Guide to Sex Addiction* (2017), 'undefended honesty' by both partners is critical for rebuilding trust and intimacy. And that honesty means being vulnerable and sharing our flaws and weaknesses, not hiding them.

The addiction explanation letter (addicted partner)

This is your opportunity explain why you became addicted to sex and/or porn; if you're not able to answer this question yet, at least in part, then you definitely need more time for therapy. There is no way that trust can be rebuilt until you can answer this question; after all, if you don't know why you did it in the first place, how can you be confident that it won't happen again? Your answer to this question should include the following:

- What issues in your childhood and adolescence contributed to the problem
- What faulty core beliefs and negative emotions were you trying to escape from
- What your key triggers were
- What you gained from acting out; for example, attention, validation, escape, excitement
- What cognitive distortions were used that enabled you to continue your behaviour
- What you did within the relationship to ensure your partner didn't find out, such as gaslighting, acting perfect, focusing on your partner's faults, being withdrawn

- What your recovery plan involves – including how you'll avoid triggers, your relapse prevention strategies and how you're working on underlying issues. This should also include sharing your relapse prevention plan, and/or, for those in 12-Step, your three-circle boundary plan.

As you write this, you need to be sure you are taking full responsibility for your behaviour, not making excuses or casting blame. This is an opportunity for an explanation – not justification. The goal is simply for you to share with your partner what you have learned through recovery; you cannot control how your partner will respond to this or make them understand.

The explanation acknowledgement letter (partner)

Once you have heard, or read, the addicted partner's explanation letter, you have the opportunity to respond to what you've heard, as well as provide information on what you have learned on your recovery journey. If you've read the above, you'll know that this letter is not an excuse for your addicted partner's behaviour. They chose to act out, they could have managed their issues another way. You may find yourself getting angry with the explanation, especially if issues within your relationship are part of it, but remember just because it is true for them, doesn't mean it has to be for you also. Reaching a shared understanding of the problem is part of your journey as a couple and this is a key element of that journey. If you find you're unable to reach a sense of meaning that both of you can tolerate, then the relationship might not survive, but you have to hear it in order to discover that. As always, working through this in therapy or with a support partner will help you to feel safe as you go through this process and respond in a healthy way, rather than react in a purely emotional way. Your acknowledgement letter should include the following:

- *Acknowledgement* – repeating back key themes to demonstrate you have heard why your addicted partner believes they became addicted
- *Empathy* – expressing that you hear the emotional difficulties your addicted partner has experienced and how they have contributed to the problem of addiction

- *Your contribution* – any areas where you're aware that you contributed to the addicted partner's feelings, whether that was through your communication, not being fully present in the relationship, being controlling or too easy-going. Please note, you may have many justifiable reasons why you behaved in some of these ways – there is plenty of time to work through that later, this is simply about acknowledging that you were part of the relationship.
- *Why you didn't know sooner* – again, this is not about blaming you, but rather acknowledging that something between the two of you enabled the behaviours to continue, things that both of you will want to change moving forward. For example, perhaps you have a tendency to avoid conflict, or to become hysterical if things are difficult. Or maybe you've been distracted by work or children or you have a tendency to trust too easily.

It may take some time to write this response and some of it may be difficult to do. It's not about blame, it's about finding a shared meaning of how this happened to your relationship, and by knowing that, what you can do to ensure it never happens again.

Task three – sharing what you need

If your relationship is going to survive, you will need to respect, and agree, to each other's recovery needs. Using our boat metaphor, this is where each of you is saying 'I am not getting back into our relation-ship without at least a life jacket'. This exercise involves both of you considering what you need from your partner, and from the relationship, in order to continue in your recovery. For partners this is about protecting themselves from triggers, wherever possible, and rebuilding their sense of safety, and for addicted partner it's also about protecting themselves from triggers, where possible, establishing effective relapse prevention strategies and confident recovery. Using our boat metaphor, this is about each of you sharing what you need to be safe in your individual cabin. If you choose to stay together, there will of course be a joint cabin too, but we will look at that in Chapter 14. Here we're focusing on your 'individual' needs in terms of addiction and trauma recovery, the boundaries that you need to establish so you can both move on from the addiction, whether that's together or apart.

Accountability and boundaries are often confused. In Chapter 4 we talked about how you can establish accountability to help both of you through the impact stage and we'll talk more about this when we come to Rebuilding Trust in Chapter 13. Here we're talking about your personal boundaries for your individual recovery. It can be helpful to think of boundaries as the central reservation in a motorway. It's an essential way of avoiding a crash, but those boundaries may at times be moved if necessary and if and when circumstances change. Setting boundaries is an essential way for each of you to protect yourselves. The most effective boundaries are practical ones that are simple to maintain and obvious to everyone. Your boundaries may be around things such as:

- *Physical contact* – couples vary enormously in how much physical and sexual contact they want. If you want to continue to sleep in separate rooms and have no physical contact, then that is a boundary that either of you can put in place. However, you can't insist on physical contact unless your partner also wants it.

- *Emotional contact* – couples also need to consider individually how they will continue to communicate on emotional matters as they move forward. For example, you may want to put a firm boundary around the extent of anger that is shown. You can't demand that your partner doesn't get angry with you, but you can set a boundary that says you do not want to be shouted at or called names. This might also include a boundary around where and when conversations take place.

- *Your home environment* – most couples will have triggers, some will be shared, others will be specific to each of you. In your individual therapy you will have identified triggers, many of which may be linked to your home environment, such as television viewing and use of Internet devices – this is where you can share your boundaries around what you need.

- *Your family and friends* – some friends and family members can be an essential support, but if there are certain people that either of you find particularly difficult to be around, then you will need to share that with each other. This may only be a temporary boundary, but if it's important to you right now, for example not to see in-laws or certain friends, then this is your opportunity to share it.

- *Your joint finances* – most couples find it helpful to set boundaries around their finances and might agree that no withdrawals are made without a partner's knowledge and both bank and credit card statements are made available.
- *Work* – if acting out has happened around the workplace, this can be a particularly difficult boundary to be drawn. If you have strong feelings that, for example, you must be allowed to travel for business, or you absolutely do not want any business travel to be allowed, now is the time to share it.
- *Alone time* – if it's particularly important for your individual recovery that you continue to have time for a particular sport, or hobby, or seeing someone socially on your own, then this is a need you can express and ask to be respected.
- *Recovery work* – this is where you can ask for what you need in terms of support from your partner for your recovery work. That might mean continuing in individual therapy, attending support groups, having privacy to make support calls to recovery companions.

As you share your boundary lists with each other, remember to use the constructive communication techniques discussed earlier. It's inevitable that you may disagree on some of your boundary requests and that you may need further explanation from each other for why this is important. If you disagree on some, first try to see if you can find a compromise, or talk it through with a couple therapist. If you can't, and your boundary is essential for you, then you might consider a temporary compromise and reconsider later. Ultimately, as a partner, your safety and stability is more important than the relationship, and if your partner can't understand that, then the relationship may not work. And if you're the one with the addiction, then you need to put your recovery before the relationship, and indeed, failing to do that means you're more likely to relapse and hence the relationship will fail anyway. At times this is going to create an inevitable paradox, especially for partners: while understandably you want your addicted partner to prove that you are the most important thing in their life, if you want to trust them again, you need to respect that their recovery must come first, even if it hurts you, because failing to recover will hurt you even more.

Before moving on to our final chapter in Part II, I'll leave you with some words of advice and support from those who responded to the couples survey.

Work things out in your own head before bringing it into the relationship. (Partner)

Don't let things slide. (Partner)

Don't avoid conflict. (Addicted partner)

I don't have to nag – perhaps helped by the fact that I get things clear in my head and consider what outcome I'd like before I communicate anything important with him. (Partner)

Don't get personal and score points. Less blaming, far more likely to say sorry, more open and likely to share how I'm feeling. More aware of how our communication impacts each other. (Addicted partner)

Take time to understand the other person's viewpoint even if it doesn't seem rational. Through this process emotions will be all over the place and things will get said that aren't necessarily true. So try not to overreact but let the situation settle first. (Addicted partner)

I've always hated conflict and letting others down so I find it hard to be honest sometimes with how I'm feeling or what I'm thinking. But that has improved and I'm slowly finding my confidence and voice. (Addicted partner)

Our communication has massively improved but I think that's because as awful as it has been it has also empowered me and I feel like I can speak up more. In the past I would be worried about saying something that upset him but now I feel like I can be more honest about how I feel and what I want. (Partner)

We do not talk late at night – especially after drinking alcohol. We use rules – leave if upset but come back to discuss the issue. Admit hurt, apologise, ALWAYS ask for forgiveness. (Partner)

We are both hypersensitive and hypervigilant to both verbal and non-verbal cues so it can feel like walking on eggshells and emotions remain raw. This means conversations can get out of hand. This happens less frequently now. (Partner)

Expect communication to be difficult for a long time. Assume partners will have lots of questions. Addicts may try to convince themselves that lying will protect the partner but it won't in the long run. Triggers (for partners) will be omnipresent and you have to work together to deal with them. (Addicted partner)

I am more able to communicate with my partner about negative things but I still have a long way to go. In the main we are much better, or at least, I believe we are. (Addicted partner)

Facing conflict in our relationship prior to discovery was very difficult. Conflict since disclosure has been much better we can still get into difficult discussions and I still have a tendency to want to walk away from it. In the main, it is better. (Partner)

This is hard and it is inevitable. From an addict's perspective I would do anything to avoid conflict which I now realise was a dangerous thing. I still have that deep desire to avoid any kind of conflict, I have to work hard to face it and work through it with my partner. In every other area of my life the ability to deal with conflict and to communicate more effectively has been enhanced significantly. It takes practice and I would say from my experience that partners have little patience with an addict who is working at it. The literature is also very aggressive in loading yet more guilt onto damaged and mentally fragile addicts. To get better at this feedback and supportive communication are essential, partners do not necessarily have those traits available to them in this stage of recovery. (Addicted partner)

References

Baucom, D.H., Snyder, D.K., Gordon, K.C. (2011) *Helping Couples Get Past the Affair – a clinician's guide*. New York: The Guilford Press.
Collins, P.C., Collins, G.N. (2017) *A Couples Guide to Sexual Addiction – A step by step plan to rebuild trust and restore intimacy*. New York: Adams Media.

Chapter 8

Considering the decision to stay or leave

Now we've reached the end of Part II our focus turns to whether you believe there is enough of your relation-ship left to salvage or if it would be better, or preferable, to walk away.

Ending a relationship is not a decision to be taken lightly, especially if you have children, and it's not one that anyone else can make for you. This chapter will not tell you what you should do, but it will give you some questions to consider to help you get closer to a decision. It takes two people to make a relationship work but only one to end it, and because the process of decision-making will be different for the partner and the person with the addiction, this chapter has questions relevant to both of you, and questions specifically for partners, and the person with the addiction. We will start with the questions that are common to you both.

Questions common to both

1. *Are you still able to enjoy each other's company?* If in spite of the addiction, you're still able to communicate in a healthy and meaningful way and you still enjoy being together, then you have a good solid basis from which to grow. Of course, it may be that it's difficult to be companionable at the moment, but if this had been something that was there in the past, it may be something worth saving.

2. *On a good day, do you feel as if there are good things in your relationship that are important to you that you don't want to lose?* This question is asking you to think about the aspects of being a couple that are particularly important to you. That might be shared parenting or other family commitments, or it may be

a business venture, your home or a shared passion. If you did separate, what might you lose that is really important to you?

3. *Would staying together mean losing something really important to you?* This is the opposite of the question above. If staying in your relationship with someone in recovery, or as someone in recovery, would mean giving up something really important to you such as certain friends, hobbies or sexual behaviours, then you may decide it's not worth the sacrifice.

4. *Do you like each other?* Whether you're a partner, or the person with the addiction, are you able to say that, in spite of the addiction, you still like each other as people? Another way of thinking about this is if you met for the first time today, would you like each other and want to spend time getting to know each other?

5. *Do you respect each other?* Similar to the question above, in spite of the addiction, are there things about each other that you still respect? For some couples, the discovery of the addiction, or the way a partner responds to the discovery, means the loss of the respect that they once had. If that's true for you, then it may be that your relationship cannot survive.

6. *Do you have a shared definition of what intimacy means?* Intimacy is important for any relationship to survive, and while intimacy may be difficult at the moment, if you don't have a shared definition of what it is, then you'll struggle to rebuild it in the future. Intimacy may include physical affection, shared responsibilities, communicating emotions, being vulnerable, sharing spirituality, being sexual together – or indeed, all of the above. What does intimacy mean to you and does your partner share your view?

7. *Do you share the same values?* The deceit that surrounds addiction and the aftermath of discovery or disclosure often means that people are not living by their value system. That can be changed, but if you don't share the same values in the first place, then staying together might mean compromising on what you believe in.

8. *Do you share the same goals for the future?* A successful long-term couple relationship needs to share the same goals and vision of what the future will look like for them, whether that's starting a family, retiring to the sun, building your own home or travelling the world. If you're not heading in the same direction, then it may be time to start different journeys.

9. *Are you scared of being alone?* Fear of being alone keeps many people trapped in painful relationships and it's never the right reason for staying together. If the only thing keeping you in this relationship is fear of loneliness, then it would be good to discuss this in therapy and begin building a wider network of friends who would be there for you if choose to separate.

10. *Are you assuming that if you get into another relationship, it would be easier or better than this one?* Some people end a relationship because they're sure 'the grass must be greener'. If you're the betrayed partner, then hopefully that wouldn't happen again in a new relationship, but it might bring other problems. And indeed, we can never guarantee that we would meet someone else who we want to be in a relationship with. If you choose to separate, then you have to be comfortable being alone, for as long as that might be.

11. *Are there signs of improvement?* If your relationship is already better than it was two months ago, or six months ago, then maybe it will be better still in another two or six months. There are no guarantees that it will continue to improve, but if you're heading in the right direction it may be worth sticking at it for longer before you make a decision.

12. *Are you willing to give more?* This is a crucial question. If you're not willing to listen more, talk more, empathise more, compromise more, grow more – then it will be very difficult to find meaningful change within your relationship. In the early stages post-disclosure or discovery, the addicted partner undoubtedly is the one who needs to give most, and that might continue for many years, but both of you need to be willing to change if your relationship is going to survive. Both addiction and recovery changes a relationship, and both of you must be willing to accommodate those changes.

Questions for the partner

1. *Does your partner accept that they are struggling with sex or porn addiction?* If your partner does not accept that they have an addiction, then they will not get into recovery and it will be impossible to rebuild trust. They may still be in denial that this is an addiction, or indeed, perhaps they are not addicted and what you're facing is a significant difference in perspective and perhaps your value system. Either way, if you don't have a shared

definition of the problem it will be very difficult to move on from it together.

2. *Have you had full disclosure?* If you haven't yet had full disclosure, then you probably won't have sufficient facts to base a decision about your future on. Furthermore, it means that your partner may not yet be able to be honest and open with you, which is essential for rebuilding your relationship.

3. *Assuming the answer is yes to the above, are you willing to accept that their behaviour is a consequence of addiction?* In other words, do you believe that that the sexual behaviours that have damaged your relationship are a consequence of the addiction, rather than something else? In other words, assuming your partner gets into recovery, are you confident that those behaviours will cease, or will at least be managed in a much healthier way?

4. *Do you understand what recovery means to your partner?* Everybody's recovery journey is different and will involve a range of strategies and some of those will have an impact on you. For example, if they're in a 12-Step fellowship, they will be going to regular meetings and need to make, and take, confidential phone calls. Or they may feel recovery means making more time for relaxing hobbies, changing their job or even moving home. Are you aware of the changes that will impact you and are you willing to support them?

5. *Are you willing to accept your partner's recovery needs within the relationship?* This question is similar to the above, but the emphasis is on what changes they believe they need within the relationship. For example, if your partner is saying that spending more time together, or apart, or developing more activities together, or working together on improving your emotional and physical intimacy is an important part of their recovery, are you willing to support this? You may not feel ready to do some of this right now, but in principle, are you willing at some stage in the future?

6. *Can you see evidence of your partner's recovery?* Can you see concrete evidence that your partner is actively working on their recovery, rather than simply saying they have stopped? For example, are they attending therapy and/or group meetings? Are they taking a proactive approach to managing stress or getting a better work/life balance? Are they more present with you and better able to manage their emotions?

7. *Can you empathise with your partner's addiction?* In the early stages after discovery, empathising with the addicted partner is, understandably, very difficult indeed. Empathy doesn't mean you understand, and certainly not that you think it was OK, but it means you're able to put yourself in someone else's shoes and accept the pain and struggles they have faced, and indeed, as an addict, may continue to face. It's difficult when you've been hurt, but it means being able to say, and believe, 'this is difficult for you too'.

8. *Are you still angry or hurt most of the time?* Making a decision about the future of your relationship will inevitably be guided by your emotions, but it should not be based on it. If you still find yourself regularly in a state of high emotion then now is not the time to make a decision that will affect both you, and those you love, for the rest of your life. Give yourself more time for these strong feelings to subside before you make the decision.

9. *Are you willing to forgive your partner?* We will talk much more about forgiveness in Chapter 12, but before you start thinking about forgiveness, you need to be willing to do it. Forgiveness is a process, not a one-off event, and it takes time. It doesn't mean that everything is OK, but that you're willing to let go of the desire for punishment and retribution. When the time is right, will you be willing to do this? If not, then staying together will be purgatory for you both.

10. *Are you willing to forgive yourself?* This may seem like an odd question for a partner and many feel they have nothing to be forgiven for, but others do blame themselves. Some continue to tell themselves that if they'd been a better partner, or if they'd been wiser and more observant, this wouldn't have happened. And some blame themselves for ever choosing the addicted partner in the first place. Any level of unforgiveness will not only damage you, but also your relationship if you choose to stay (much more on forgiveness in Chapter 12).

11. *Do you 'want' to be able to trust again?* Chapter 13 is all about trust, what it is and how you begin to rebuild it, but if you've already made a decision that you don't ever 'want' to trust your partner again, then it may be better for both of you to separate. Trust is essential for a relationship to thrive and also for partners to regain some stability in their lives – are you willing to try and trust again?

12. *Are you confident you can ask for your needs to be met to move on from this?* There will be many things, emotional and practical, that will need to change to enable you to recover from the trauma of betrayal; are you aware of what those needs are for you? For example, that may be more affection or more time together, greater empathy or more open conversations. You can't at this stage guarantee if those needs will be met, but do you know what they are and are you confident enough to ask for them?

13. *Are you willing to take responsibility for the areas in your relationship where you need to change?* As we saw in Chapter 6, many relationships have difficulties before the tidal wave of addiction hits – as you worked through the exercises were you able to see where you could have behaved differently and are you willing to make changes within yourself to improve your relationship if you stay together? If you believe all of your relationship problems were due to the addiction, and your partner disagrees, then it's unlikely you'll be able to work together to make your relationship a happy one.

14. *Miracle question – if you were offered a magic pill that would mean that nobody would be hurt if you left the relationship and nobody would look unfavourably on you, would you take it?* This question gives you the opportunity to look at whether you might be choosing to stay in the relationship for the wrong reasons. In other words, are you considering staying because you're frightened of hurting other people or because you fear what others may think of you if you end it? If you choose to stay, it has to be because the decision is right for you.

In my survey, I asked the couples how close they had got to seriously deciding to end their relationship, and mark on a scale of 0–10, with 0 being not at all and 10 being very close. This is what some of the partners said:

Scored 5: I thought that the relationship would come to a horrible end as I believed initially that I was a cover for his 'deviant' behaviour. The relationship has never been better now, but paradoxically almost, my safety comes first. If he put that in jeopardy again, I would leave the relationship.

Scored 0.5: The shared experiences outside of the addiction were often mutually good, why give them up?

Scored 9: At first I couldn't ever see a way through that ended in us still being together and we did separate for a couple of months. Things are really good at the moment, but there are still times though when I get really worried about being hurt again and feel like running away from it all. These times are getting less as time goes on.

Scored 10: I think about ending the relationship many, many times each day as the effort of trying to rebuild seems overwhelming. I'm concerned that my need to be needed is preventing me from making a clear decision.

Scored 10: When I realised for a further 6 months he was still addicted and had a major remission. But now we've worked through it – mainly for our kids. I have also now brought him down from the pedestal I put him on. He is human and makes mistakes.

Questions for the addicted partner

1. *Do you accept you have sex or porn addiction?* If you're still in doubt whether your behaviour stemmed from sex or porn addiction, or from something else, then you're not in the right place to make a decision about the future of your relationship. You may prefer to use a different name, such as compulsivity, but nonetheless, do you agree that the behaviour stemmed from this? If you and your partner cannot agree on what the problem is, then it's unlikely you'll be able to rebuild your relationship.

2. *Are you 'fully' in recovery?* Assuming you do accept the term addiction, or compulsion, are you in recovery or have you just stopped? Getting into recovery means you will have learnt about the underlying drivers of your behaviour and be working on those as well as on pragmatic relapse prevention strategies. It means you'll be active in your recovery and building a new life for yourself. If you're not fully in recovery it will be very difficult to rebuild trust and move forward.

3. *Have you accepted full responsibility for your addiction?* If you're still blaming something else for your behaviour, especially if it's your relationship, then you're probably not yet in the right place to make a decision. Undoubtedly other things in your life will

have contributed to the addiction, including problems within your relationship, but nonetheless, you have to take full responsibility for the choices you made in the past and the decisions you make for the future.

4. *Is sex a significant main driver for your decision?* While sex in a relationship is important, it should not be the main reason for either leaving or staying. There is much more to a relationship than sex and you need to be confident that your decision is based on a whole relationship, not just part of it.

5. *Have you made a full disclosure?* If you are still holding on to significant secrets, then that probably means you're scared of the relationship ending if your partner learnt the truth. As discussed in Chapter 5, without full disclosure, you will never be able to trust that your partner is staying with you because of who you are, or because of who they think you are. If you choose to stay in the relationship without full disclosure, your relationship will continue to be tainted by fears of discovery and self-doubt.

6. *Can you empathise with your partner?* If you're unable to accept the very real pain and trauma that your partner has experienced due to your behaviours, and be willing to demonstrate that you know how they feel, then even if you do choose to stay, your partner will continue to doubt you or make the decision to leave. As we saw in the last chapter, empathy is essential for healing a couple relationship, so if you think they're just over-reacting, it might be wiser to walk away now.

7. *Can you accept that your partner will never 'get over this'?* While many addicts do understand and empathise with their partner's pain, they often stay because they assume that one day they'll 'get over it'. This is like thinking that someone who loses a loved one will 'get over' his or her death. Hopefully the hole in their life that your betrayal caused will get smaller in proportion to other areas of growth, but it will never disappear. Deciding to stay will mean accepting that your partner may always be triggered, hopefully less and less often, but when they are, the pain may feel as bad as what you see today.

8. *Are you willing to accept your partner's recovery needs?* Hopefully your partner will have been doing their own work to recover from the trauma and will have identified changes they need in their life and within your relationship to help them to heal. This will almost certainly include accountability measures, as explained in Chapter 4, but may also include changes in the way

you operate as a couple or requesting that you change your job or move home. Before you make a decision to stay, be sure you know what your partner needs from you and be sure you're ready to give it.

9.   *Are you confident you can ask for your needs to be met?* You will also have recovery needs, some of which may have a negative impact on your partner. For many in recovery, balancing their personal recovery with the needs of loved ones can be a challenge and if you're going to take both your recovery and your relationship seriously, then you need to be confident that you can ask for what you need, even if it's going to cause conflict.

10.   *Is your partner willing to accept and try to meet your recovery needs?* Having identified your needs for recovery, is your partner willing to try and meet them? This may range from practical things such as the personal space to do recovery activities, go to meetings and make outreach calls or time to build friendships or start new hobbies, but also emotional matters such as rebuilding intimacy and getting close again. If your partner is unwilling to do this, then no matter how much you want the relationship to work, it probably won't. Or if it does, it may cost you your recovery.

11.   *Are you willing to forgive yourself?* In the last chapter we talked about how loving yourself is one of the ground rules for a successful relationship and this is something that many people with addiction struggle with, especially after disclosure. You may be struggling to forgive yourself at the moment, but if you've decided you never will, then you could be making a decision about your relationship based on the wrong criteria. Some people stay in a broken relationship out of penance for what they've done, others leave because they can't face the pain they've caused their partner. When you forgive yourself and let go of your mistakes, you can be more confident you're staying or leaving for the right reasons.

12.   *Are you willing to forgive your partner?* There may not be anything you feel you need to forgive your partner for, in which case this question is not relevant, but if you're bearing a grudge that your partner could in some way have prevented your addiction, or intervened sooner, or you continue to be angry at how they made the discovery or things they've done as a consequence, then whether you decide to leave or stay, you need to let this go. You'll find more on forgiveness in Chapter 12.

13. *Thinking back to when your relationship was at its happiest, could you be that happy again now you're not acting out?* So this is a question that should help you to think about how big a role your addiction has played in your satisfaction in your relationship. Your answer may instantly be that if you didn't have the addiction, your relationship would have been much, much, much happier. However, if your answer is that in some ways it was your addiction that led you to get into the relationship, or kept you in it even though you weren't sure if it was working, then you may find the relationship doesn't improve now you're in recovery.

14. *The miracle question – if you had a magic wand and one wish could be granted, which wish would you prefer: (1) your partner would be 100% OK with you leaving and build a wonderful future for themselves, or (2) your partner would forget all of your acting out behaviours and trust you again?* This is a question to help you think about your true motivation in deciding to leave or stay. If you would wish for (1), then perhaps the only reason you're staying is guilt and shame and that is never a sound basis for a decision. If you would wish for (2), then it's worth staying and working at it.

In the survey, when the person with the addiction was asked how close they had got to seriously deciding to end their relationship, this is what they said:

> Scored: 7–8 when emotions ran high, 1–2 at other times – when I felt overwhelmed by wife's anger and rage I did sometimes feel that I couldn't go on and handle what felt like a constant barrage of shouting – almost certainly took me back to painful childhood experiences. But when not under attack, then I wanted the relationship to work more than anything else. Sometimes now I feel I can't get away from the past despite being a very different person now. This doesn't occur very often, but the feelings are so intense that I think leaving is the only way out at the time – fortunately my recovery network provides a good anchor during these moments of 'insanity'.

> Scored 0: Never entered my thinking.

> Scored 10: When I disclosed I was certain that would be the end of the relationship. It was a shock when I first realised that there was a chance of reconciliation.

Scored 9: Recently I have felt that the damage caused to my partner is such that it is not repairable. I have no doubt that a new start would in many ways be a much easier scenario for me. I also think that the new version me would like to feel valued for being me. In this relationship I feel that this will never be enough; whilst this is entirely understandable it is a negative factor that it may be better to not have in my life. I can never make the past better only the future and the now.

Final considerations

Hopefully these questions will have helped you in the process of making a decision, but as well as the emotional and psychological issues, there are also many practical ones. Some people simply can't afford to separate, while others know it would be a significant strain on both individual and personal circumstances. In the short term, the cost of separation may be too great and hence staying together may make more sense. Furthermore, there are the needs of children to consider: what the impact will be on them if you stay together and if you separate.

There is absolutely no rush to make a final decision about your relationship. Many couples find themselves being hassled by friends and relatives to make a decision, but there is no reason to let other people's sense of haste create a sense of urgency in you. One couple in the survey have been living separately for over a year, while they each continue on their individual recovery and explore their relationship in couple therapy. If you're not sure what you want, then wait. Make an active, positive decision to postpone making a final decision until you feel clearer about whether your relationship can survive. Using our boat analogy, it may be impossible to know if your relation-ship can become sea-worthy again before starting on some of the repairs. You can't stay in dry dock forever, but you can start slowly, maybe checking first if your relation-ship can float, then ensuring you stay close to the harbour before the final relaunch. And remember, choosing to stay together does not mean that you can't bail out of the ship later if things don't work. Let me leave the final words to one of our partners:

Our relationship has experienced post-traumatic growth. It's far, far better than we had before, and, indeed, any relationship that I could even imagine. I would like to say to couples in recovery/healing from this trauma, 'please don't leave before the miracle happens'. (Partner)

Trial separation

Some couples find that a trial separation for an agreed amount of time gives them the distance they need to clarify their thinking. Moving out of a highly charged emotional situation may provide you both with the space you need to focus on your own individual recovery and consider your future. If you choose this option, it's important that you're clear about the purpose of the separation and have communicated that with each other. You'll also need to think about whether and how you'll communicate with each other during the break. And of course, what you'll tell children if you have them.

Considering children's needs

Deciding to stay 'for the sake of the children' is often thought as not being a good reason to stay, but if you love your children, of course you're going to worry about what impact separation would have on them. In Chapter 10 we talk a lot more about how children are affected by separation, and the essentials of co-parenting, but if you stay together in an unhappy relationship, that will impact them as well. Children learn about relationships from what they see their parents do, and what they see that they don't do. Whichever decision you make, it will impact your children. However, if you both feel strongly that separating now would be particularly detrimental to your children, for example, if they've recently started a new school or are taking exams or are vulnerable in another way, then that's a very good reason to postpone making a decision.

Summary for couple therapists – the meaning stage

The focus of the meaning stage is to develop a shared understanding of why the addiction occurred and what this means to the couple relationship. For some couples the process of therapeutic disclosure throws them temporarily back into impact, but generally couples begin to be ready to explore meaning after approximately 6 months post initial disclosure or discovery. Like the impact stage, emotions may still be running high, but with more individual coping skills developed, the therapist's task is to encourage clients to explore what's left of their relationship and what would be required if the relationship is to continue. With many clients still unsure if they want the relationship to survive, this is also the time to consider options for divorce or separation. During this phase therapy should focus on:

- Facilitating a therapeutic disclosure
- Helping each individual within the couple to share their thoughts and feelings about the addiction
- Exploring relationship satisfaction before discovery or disclosure to help clients consider if they wish to save the relationship
- Helping clients to identify problems within their relationship that are not a direct consequence of the addiction that they may wish to work on
- Encouraging the partner to establish and communicate boundaries and to engage in self-care strategies when triggered
- Encouraging the addicted partner to continue to demonstrate 'relentless empathy'

- Ensuring there is ongoing honest and open communication around accountability
- Continuing to minimise conflict and shame
- Continuing to build healthy patterns of communication
- Encouraging couples to take self-responsibility and build compassion for themselves and each other
- Helping individuals within the couple to consider the option of separation

Part III

Re-launching your life – alone

We begin now to talk about moving on and Part III is all about what moving on means if you have decided to separate. Separating is never an easy decision, and regrettably it's rarely one where both partners within the relationship agree. So you might be reading this chapter reluctantly, having discovered that your partner has decided that your relation-ship is never going to re-launch together, or you may be reading it because the decision is yours. In our first chapter, Chapter 9, we focus on how you can ensure that you have a healthy divorce; one where you can manage difficult emotions and focus on building a positive future for yourself alone. If you have children, you'll find lots of information and advice in Chapter 10 on how to minimise any negative impact on them and how to continue your co-parenting relationship.

Chapter 9

Having a 'healthy' divorce

You may be reading this chapter because either you, or your partner, have already made the decision that you should separate. Or you may be reading it because you're considering if separation is the best option for you or because you know, or suspect, that's what your partner is thinking. Either way, what follows is a brief guide on how to separate in a way that can minimise the distress to yourself and your family.

Divorce and separation is never an easy option; it will mark a significant turning point in your life, but if you manage it in a healthy way, it can be a stepping stone to a better future – even if it was a decision that's been forced on you. If your main concern is the impact separating will have on your children, then you'll also find advice and guidance on how to support them through the turbulent process, minimise harmful effects and help them to look forward to a new, stable, re-formed family life.

During my 18 years working for Relate, initially as a couple counsellor and then later as a family therapist, I learnt a lot about divorce and separation and also the impact it has on children. While working for Relate I also wrote the Relate Guide, *How to Have a Healthy Divorce* (Hall, 2008). Much of what follows is taken from this book, and although it was written 10 years ago, the process and the impact of separation has not changed. It is still one of the most stressful and painful experiences that anyone will go through, but for many, the pain is better than staying in a broken or dead relationship. If you choose to separate, then this will be the end of the line for your couple relation-ship, but it's not the end of the line for you as individuals, and certainly not as parents. People can, and do, rebuild their lives after divorce; families are reshaped and integrated in different ways. The journey of life continues.

How to have a healthy divorce

Although having a healthy divorce or separation is difficult, it is not impossible and largely the decision about how you face your new future is up to you. You can feel empty, anxious, broken and resentful for the rest of your life, or you can choose to overcome the wounds of divorce and become happy and whole again. Many people struggle with divorce because our emotions often tell us to behave in ways that are detrimental to our well-being. Anger may push people way and make us defensive; grief can overwhelm us and leave us feeling powerless; fear can stop us from taking the necessary risks to grow and move on and feelings of guilt and rejection may tell us we don't deserve to feel any better than this. However, like the struggles of having an addiction and the trauma of discovering your loved one is addicted to sex or porn, these are emotions that can be conquered, and once achieved, you can face your future with optimism and confidence. What follows is a five-step plan to help you have the healthiest divorce possible. Of course, it does take two people to make that intention a reality, but you can endeavour to do everything within your power to encourage that.

Step I – accept the reality of your situation

Over the previous months you will undoubtedly have both questioned if your relationship could survive, but nonetheless, once the decision to separate has been made, it can still come as a shock. Even if it was you who made the decision, the reality of the choice you've made may still leave you feeling numb and confused for some time. Nobody wants their relationship to end, and therefore it's natural to struggle to come to terms with all the ramifications of the final decision. Ending a relationship means also means letting go of any hopes of reconciliation and saying goodbye to the many things you shared together, as well as your hopes and dreams for the future. We invest so much of ourselves into our relationships and it's often not until a relationship is over that we realise how vast the challenge of separation can be as we're confronted with the task of unravelling all the knots that bind us together. Those knots include emotional things such as a shared love of your children and your home as well as practical things like financial responsibilities, childcare and home maintenance. Many couples will have enjoyed a shared social life or career and had joint plans for the future. Of course, the previous months of coming to terms with addiction and betrayal will already have impacted much of this, but nonetheless, realising that you're saying goodbye to that forever is still tough. It's commonplace for the partner who didn't initiate the separation to assume that the decision has been reached because the other either is still not fully in recovery, or hasn't worked through their trauma. But even if that is true, holding onto 'they'll change their mind' will impede both of you in moving forward. If you're right, then the decision can be reversed, but for now you need to accept this is where you are today and you are separating.

Accepting that it's over is also essential before you even consider telling your children. They may already know, or have worked out, that there are problems between you, but before you say anything, you need to have confirmed what your separation will mean for them. When one parent is saying it's over and another says we're working things out, it can create significant additional stress and anxiety for children. There's much more on helping children later in the next chapter.

Step 2 – manage your emotions

There's no doubt that both of you will have done a considerable amount of work on managing emotion in your individual recovery journeys, but what we're talking about here are the emotions that are specific to divorce and separation. If the decision to separate has been forced on you, you may struggle more with your recovery, or you may experience it as an additional trauma. Either way, you'll need additional support to continue in the progress you've already made and work through the additional emotional challenges that separating will inevitably bring. We will look at the key emotions now.

- *Grief and fear* – when a relationship ends there is more to grieve than simply the loss of the relationship. For many people, separating also means losing an important part of their identity, being a wife, or husband or resident parent. It may also mean losing your home and some possessions, your standard of living and you may also lose the relationship you had with your in-laws and some of your friends. Many people understandably fear being alone, and also the impact of the separation on children, other family members and friends. And indeed for many, the impact on their partner. One of the best strategies for managing these emotions is firstly simply to acknowledge them. Many people find it helpful to write down what they may lose and the subsequent fears and talk through with a therapist or friend. In the process, many fears prove to be unfounded, or at least you have the opportunity to look at how to overcome or avoid them. You may also find it beneficial to write down the things that you 'won't' miss. Even if you're not the one who initiated the separation, no relationship is perfect and undoubtedly you would have faced many challenges if you'd continued together, so making a note of benefits, as well as losses, can help to soothe the pain.
- *Anger and resentment* – anger is a natural and common response to any kind of loss, and as we've seen, there are many losses when couples separate. The anger may be directed at yourself, especially if you blame yourself for the breakdown of the relationship. Or it may be directed at your partner for giving up, at a therapist who couldn't 'save' your relationship, or even more broadly at authorities or society for not preventing this or giving you the support that you wanted. And when anger is not faced and managed healthily, it can fester into resentments and bitterness. Although anger may be inevitable, it is your choice how you respond to it and express it. Many people hold on to anger because they want to punish themselves or their partner, or because they think it will protect them from being hurt again. But in reality, all it does is keep you emotionally bound to your painful past. When we can work through anger and begin to let it go, we can be free to move forward in our lives.

- *Doubt, regret and guilt* – many people think that it will only be the person who chose to end the relationship who may feel doubt, but it's common for both partners to wonder if the right decision has been made and wonder if there is more they could have done. Regret is also common – 'could I have done more?', 'what if ...'. If unchecked, doubt and regret can add to feelings of guilt, telling you 'I *should* have done more' and 'if only ...'. Ending a relationship is a life-changing decision, not just for each of you, but also for everyone who cares about you, so doubts are inevitable. Ultimately no-one knows the future and what would have happened 'if' you had done something else; therefore, the best way to manage doubts is to refuse to dwell on them and rather to remind yourself that you did the best you could at the time, and the past cannot be changed, only the future.

Step 3 – assess your strengths, skills and support opportunities

Going through the separation process and building a new life on your own, or as a single parent, is going to require additional resources to the ones you needed when you were in a relationship. Some of those resources will be practical ones, such as your ability to cook, do basic DIY and manage your finances, while others will be more emotional and psychological, such as how patient you are with difficult people or how comfortable you are at social events. When we're in a relationship, especially if it's been a long one, then many responsibilities are shared and each partner learns to play to their strengths and lets the other partner manage anything they're less confident with.. Over time you may have forgotten some of the strengths and skills you have because you stopped using them, or you may have stopped valuing them because your partner was better. For example, you may have always had a good head for numbers, but if you were married to an accountant, you probably left finances to them. You may also have lost touch with some of your strengths because they weren't valued by your partner. For example, if they were critical of your quiet self-containment because they thought it was boring, or conversely they found your gregariousness loud and obtrusive. All of these hidden qualities can return and become valuable resources to you as you go through divorce and start a new life.

You will undoubtedly have overcome many challenges in the past as well, not least the addiction or the subsequent relationship trauma, but perhaps bereavements, work challenges or family issues. And you may have a string of achievements, whether that's professional or personal.

Another key resource you will have are the friends and family around you, whether they're people who can support you emotionally or socialise with, or people who can help in more practical ways such as gardening or childcare.

Creating a resources list

Writing down the resources you have at your disposal can help you to feel more prepared for whatever the future holds and minimise the risk of feeling anxious or overwhelmed. Take a sheet of paper and note down the following headings: 'psychological strengths', 'practical skills', 'friends and family' and list everything you can think of beneath. If you're struggling to do this, then consider what a close friend might say about you. Also think also about the strengths and skills you use in the workplace or that you've utilised to overcome difficulties in the past. Some of these may not seem immediately relevant, but list them anyway as you may think differently after completing Step 4.

Step 4 – consider emotional and practical challenges

Everyone's experience of divorce is different, which means each of us will face very different personal struggles and practical challenges. Indeed, something that's a struggle for one person may be liberating for another; for example, more time alone may feel liberating for one person, while for someone else it may feel more like enforced solitary confinement. But one struggle that is common for most people is missing sharing a life with someone. Even if your break up was hostile and you're confident you won't miss 'your partner', there'll still inevitably be times ahead when you'll miss just having someone around or miss some of the things you did together, and the responsibilities that were previously shared; things that perhaps you took for granted as part of being in a couple relationship. Others miss a home they've left behind or children. No one wants to leave their kids, but the reality of divorce is that one or both of you will have long periods of time when you're not with them, while they're with the other parent. Most people also find they lose some of their social circle when they separate and find it more awkward socialising as a single person; and if you were close to your in-laws, that may be another relationship that you lose, or that becomes more sensitive once you've separated.

There are other more practical challenges as well. Money will almost certainly be more limited and you may find yourself losing practical possessions that you'd hitherto assumed access to, such as a second car, a lawnmower or the coffee machine. On the surface these may seem like small things, but when you're trying to adjust to so many other changes in your life, suddenly discovering you've got to catch a bus when your car goes in for service or that you can no longer afford to make yourself a decent cup of coffee at home can feel like additional stresses and irritations you don't need. Running a home alone may also confront you with day-to-day living challenges such as keeping up with the laundry, cooking, car maintenance, paying bills, lifts for kids, computer maintenance, DIY, gardening, looking after pets – and all that may be on top of having a full-time job, or even having to take on extra work to cover the increase in living costs.

Creating a challenges list

As you've been reading the previous paragraphs you may have remembered a number of other challenges too, so now's the time to list them. Give yourself space for two columns, one headed 'emotional' and the other 'practical', and write down all the challenges that you expect to face. If you're in an optimistic mood and are tempted to leave some things off, I would recommend you write it down anyway – even if that's just so you can tick it off the list quickly and easily.

Step 5 – develop an action plan

So now you have a list of your strengths and resources, and a list of your emotional and personal challenges. The first task is to look at the practical challenges and see how many of them you can tick off with the resources you have to hand. There are a number of ways you can do this. The simplest is see that you have a strength in that area and hence don't need to worry too much, but the other way requires some lateral thinking and perhaps a little humility. If you have the financial ability, then you may be able to pay someone to make life easier, such as getting a cleaner or a gardener. You may have friends or family members who would be more than happy to help you out in some practical ways, or you can consider a skill/resource swap. For example, offering to do a mow a neighbour's lawn in exchange for them walking the dog, or lift share with other parents. If you and your ex are able to continue to collaborate, you might offer to take on additional responsibilities for childcare, or laundry, in exchange for DIY and computer maintenance. If there are particular areas where you know you may struggle and you're not sure who can help, see if you can get yourself booked onto an evening class in car maintenance or cooking, or whatever it is. Not only would evening classes increase your skills, but it will also give you the opportunity to get out of the house and meet new people. Perhaps the most important practical resource you can get is a diary and a spreadsheet. If time and/or money are limited, then planning ahead and being organised is essential. Not only to ensure you manage on a practical basis, but also to prevent you from feeling emotionally overwhelmed.

We already looked earlier at how to manage some of the emotional challenges that you're likely to face, such as feelings of fear and anger, but there are additional strategies you can consider that can support you through the early days. Over time you will get increasingly used to being alone and living life as a single person, rather than half of a couple, but that does take time – especially if you were in a relationship for many years. It can be easy to become isolated if you don't make a conscious effort to socialise and meet new people. And although 40 per cent of marriages end in divorce, it's still easy to feel that you're the only single person on the planet, especially if all your friends are still in relationships. If you have single friends, then building your relationship with them is a great starting place, but also consider joining a singles social group, or take up a new hobby where you'll meet new people. That might be something based around fitness or learning something new, or it might be joining an existing book club, volunteer group or church, or taking up amateur dramatics or singing. It really doesn't matter what you do, as long as you continue to get out into the world and live your life.

Reference

Hall, P.A. (2008) *How to Have a Healthy Divorce*. Relate guide. London: Vermillion.

Chapter 10

Helping children cope with your divorce

There is not space in this book to provide you with all the help and information you need to support your children, so do also look at one of the books I wrote for Relate, *Help Your Children Cope with Your Divorce* (Hall, 2007). Children of all ages are affected by divorce, but they don't have to be devastated by it. The way a child is affected will depend on their age, but regrettably there really is no 'good' age for parents to separate. Even a baby or small child who is too young to understand what's going on can pick up on a parent's distress; it's common for this age group to regress to an earlier developmental stage such as bedwetting, wanting a bottle, or taking longer to settle to sleep. Children between the ages of five and eight will have more understanding of the situation and be easier to comfort with words, but this age group can be particularly sensitive to being separated from a parent and may fear losing them for ever. The nine to 12 age group are the ones most likely to respond with anger, as they feel acutely aware of the injustice of the situation and the impact it will have on them. Over 13s have to face the emotional upheaval of separation on top of their own roller coaster of adolescent emotions, but generally they are more understanding of the complexities of relationships and the imperfections of people and the world.

All children, of any age, will experience feelings of confusion, loss, sadness, frustration and anger. All will be susceptible to taking sides to try to redress what they may see as inequality and unfairness, especially if they are hearing negative messages about the other parent, and many will try to get more control and understanding of the situation by demanding answers to why this has happened. A frightening number of children will tell themselves they could have prevented the separation in some way, and blame themselves (Amato, 2010; Mooney et al., 2009). Older children who have been told, or over-heard, about the addiction, may struggle with shock, disbelief and betrayal, as well as to self-doubt about why they didn't notice, in a similar way to partners. They may also struggle more with their own compulsive behaviours, or fear developing them.

The effects of divorce and separation on children can be far-reaching, including struggling more at school and developing behav-ioural and relationship problems, but don't lose hope, because the two major causes can be avoided. Evidence shows that it is the con-flict surrounding divorce and the quality of contact with both parents that makes the most significant difference, not the actual event of divorce itself (Cohen, 2002; Cummings & Davies, 2011; Kieran & Mensah, 2010). So, whatever the age of your children, by avoiding conflict and ensuring regular contact with both of you, you can min-imise the impact. And evidence also shows that children do survive, and indeed, can thrive (Wallerstein & Blakeslee, 2004).

It's important to remember that divorce is something that affects children's lives forever. It is not an event to be 'got through', but a permanent change to their family structure. As well as the emotional upheaval of realising your parents no longer love each other and one parent is leaving, there are also the practical changes they have to endure. For most there will be less money and perhaps a new home and new school, and new routines of trying to juggle two parents and two homes.

This is a time when your children need you to be strong, hopeful and available for them, but regrettably this coincides with what is probably the toughest time in any parent's life. Just when you may feel that you have the least emotional and practical resources to pro-vide for your children, they need it most. While you're trying to pick up the pieces of your own life, and perhaps your heart as well, your children need you to be the best parent that you can be. Parenting through divorce is perhaps the toughest challenge you'll ever face.

If you've got children then this is the bottom line. In spite of how you may be feeling emotionally, you are responsible for behaving in a way and making decisions that will always be in the best interests of your children. It doesn't matter whether you wanted the separation, or what your ex has done, or how, or who with, your children's needs must come first. That means that unless you have genuine concerns for your child's safety (which is a decision that only social services and the courts can make), your children should have contact with both of you. Maintaining a healthy relationship with 'both' parents is essential and it's up to each of you to create an environment where that is possible and encouraged.

Co-parenting communication

We've already looked at communication in previous chapters, but what follows here are additional key principles if you're going through a divorce or separation. These are communication essentials that can help to minimise the impact the decision to separate will have on your children, and they are ones that both of you need to read and agree.

- First and foremost, always separate discussions about the children from all other conversations you have with each other. Make it clear that the conversation you are having is about the children and for 'their' benefit. The children are your mutual agenda and their happiness is your mutual goal. A top tip for keeping you focused is to have a picture of your children on the table in front of you both when you talk.
- When you need to talk about the children, especially if you know it may be difficult, do not talk in front of them. Remember it's conflict and tension between parents that harms children the most. Having them out of earshot will also ensure they don't try to chip in and help!
- If it's difficult to have a constructive conversation face to face, then use the telephone or email instead. This has the additional advantage of providing each of you with a written copy of what's been said.
- When you do speak in front of the children, which will happen at handover times or school or family events you both attend, make sure you're calm and courteous and treat each other with respect – even if that's not how you feel.
- Finally, don't use your children as mediators or messengers. This puts children in an impossible position of having to remember

and convey the message accurately while delivering it in a way that won't upset the other parent. They also have to cope with the reaction from the other parent and make a decision about what to do with any spoken or unspoken information they receive.

For older children, it's also important that you quickly establish separate communication channels between each of you as parents with your children, in other words, no more family chat or family Facebook. This will help your children to feel confident in communicating openly with each parent, without being at risk of hurting the other, and also helps to establish that the relationship they have with each of you is now separate and their individual choice and responsibility.

Breaking the news

The best way to break the news of your separation is together. Even if they've suspected that you might split up for some time, or one of you has already shared your decision, the formal breaking of the news should be together. This demonstrates that you're united in your decision, even if it's reluctant on one side, and reinforces the message that you're going to be working together to find the best possible solutions for the family. We discussed how much to share with children in Chapter 5, but just a reminder here it that will depend on their age and maturity. What you do need to make clear is that it is the relationship that has broken down, not the family. You will continue to be a family, but the two of you will no longer be a couple.

Before breaking the news you need to have agreed what you're going to say and what's happening next. For example, what the new living arrangements will be; when the changes will happen; what you'll do about holidays and Christmas where the pets will live. You know your children better than anyone else, so ideally try to brainstorm the questions they're likely to ask and be ready to answer them. This will help them to feel reassured that the grown-ups are still in charge and in control.

Once you've told the children, you'll need to ensure you quickly inform other people that they know, such as grandparents, their school, other friends' parents. While children don't want to be the last to know, they also shouldn't be put in a position of keeping secrets from anyone close to them.

Establishing living and contact arrangements

When considering who will live where and how often the non-resident parent will see the children, your priority should be what your children need. Obviously, you'll need to consider geographic and financial practicalities, but experts agree that it's best to maintain as much of the status quo as you can. That means maximum access to both of you and as few changes to regular routines such as school and friends as possible.

When one or both of you is hurting or angry, it's tempting to use your children as a weapon against each other. The more committed your ex is as a parent, the more tempting it can be to use limiting contact with their children as punishment. But remember, no matter how badly you may feel you've been treated in your relationship, your ex can still be an excellent parent, whether they're in recovery from addiction or trauma. Furthermore, your children need the love and support of 'both' of you, and doing this will punish them as well as your ex.

Managing everyone's feelings

Separation is one of the most painful and distressing events that anyone will experience and it will affect everyone in the family. Wherever possible, you and your ex need to make sure that you protect your children from the overwhelming emotions you may sometimes feel. That doesn't mean you have to pretend that everything's OK, but remember that children can be frightened by strong displays of emotion that, to them, may feel out of control. Sharing that you're worried, angry or sad about what's happening can help them to feel more comfortable expressing their own feelings, but make sure you're also giving them plenty of reassurance that you're coping and life is going to be OK. Make a pact with yourself, too, that you will never put your ex down in front of your children. When you do this you're not just undermining the other parent, but also part of your children. Because they share the same genes, criticising their parent means criticising them too.

You and your ex should also agree that you will both be available to talk to the children whenever they need to. It's important to maintain an open-door policy to address their concerns and feelings over the coming weeks and months. When your children do talk to you, make sure you include the other parent in any decisions that need to be made. Children need to know that the two of you will be continuing to work together for them, and that you value and respect the other parent as a mum or a dad, even though you'll no longer be a couple.

When an ex won't or can't cooperate

Unfortunately not all parents are able to put the needs of their children above their own, or indeed recognise when their children's needs differ from their own. Often this is due to unresolved anger or guilt, or because of their very real struggle to manage their loss and come to terms with what's happened. This may also be true if your ex continues to stay in active addiction or has not had enough support in recovering from the trauma of betrayal. Your ex may seem determined to thwart your attempts to communicate, no matter how hard you try, and they may seem determined to damage the contact between you and your children, or their own relationship with them. Try not to give up and keep working on communication, but also consider talking to a third party. If your ex has a friend or family member they respect, ask them if they will act as an intermediary. If that doesn't work, you could consider trying a mediation service or, as a last resort, you may need to speak to your solicitor. Whatever course of action you take, remember that your children's needs must come first.

References

Amato, P.R. (2010) Research on divorce: continuing trends and new developments. *Journal of Marriage and Family*, *72*: 650–666.
Cohen, G.J. (2002) Helping children and families deal with divorce and separation. *Pediatrics*, *110*: 1019–1023.

Cummings, E.M., Davies, P.T. (2011) *Marital Conflict and Children: An emotional security perspective.* New York: Guilford Press.

Hall, P.A. (2007) *Help Your Children Cope with Your Divorce.* Relate guide. London: Vermillion.

Kiernan, K., Mensah, F. (2010) Partnership trajectories, parent and child well-being. In *Children of the 21st Century* (edited by K. Hansen, H. Joshi, D. Dex). Bristol: Policy Press, 77–94.

Mooney, A., Oliver, C., Smith, M. (2009) *Impact of family breakdown on children's wellbeing evidence review DCSF-RR113.* London: University of London, Institute of Education, Thomas Coram Research Unit.

Wallerstein, J.S., Blakeslee, S. (2004). *Second Chances: Men, women, and children a decade after divorce.* Boston, MA: Houghton Mifflin.

Summary for couple therapists – moving on alone

If one individual within the couple has made the decision to separate, then the focus of work for the therapist becomes how to ensure the separation causes minimal emotional and psychological damage to each partner and to any children that may be involved. Referral to mediation and/or family therapy may also be appropriate, as well as extra encouragement to continue their journeys through individual therapy or their support groups. When a decision has been made to separate, therapy should focus on:

- Ensuring the person who has made the decision to separate has considered the options fully
- If one partner is opposed to the decision, ensuring they are receiving adequate independent support to work through their grief process
- Helping each partner to accept the reality of the decision to separate and what each of them will need to do to ensure they have a 'healthy' divorce
- Encouraging the couple to see separation as an opportunity for personal growth, not as a failure
- Providing information on the most common reactions their children may experience
- Guiding the couple in how to minimise the impact on children
- Encouraging clients to develop positive co-parenting communication and continue regular contact with both parents

Further to the above, consideration should be given to directing clients to individual therapy in addition to working through divorce and separation as a couple.

Part IV

Re-launching your life – together

Part IV is all about rebuilding and re-launching your relation-ship together. In Chapter 11 each partner is guided to reflect on how they have changed as a result of the addiction and what they need from their partner as they becoming joint crew members again. Chapter 12 focuses on the difficult topic of forgiveness and how failing to let go of the pain of the past can inadvertently keep you tethered to the dock forever. Trust is the hull of your new relation-ship, and how to rebuild it is covered in Chapter 13. This chapter includes an exploration of the different domains of trust, the essential building blocks of trust and detailed advice for the addicted partner on becoming trustworthy. Part IV ends with Chapter 14, which is devoted to developing and deepening intimacy within your relation-ship. Intimacy is described as the engine, or sails, of your new relationship and you'll find practical strategies for enjoying greater intimacy in every area of your relationship, including sexual intimacy, so you can look forward to heading out to sea again.

Chapter 11

Acknowledging and accepting new roles

We have now come to the point in the book where we begin to talk about moving on together: what it means, and what's required to ensure you both enjoy a happy and satisfying relationship. This chapter is about the new roles that each of you will inevitably be playing as a consequence of the addiction.

The bottom line is this – your relation-ship will never be the same. One partner shared: *"your 'old' relationship has gone, you'll never get it back"*. That may be a relief for some, but you need to understand that there may be some elements of your new relation-ship that you will not like. The tidal wave may be over, and you may be able to completely remodel your relation-ship, but there will always be scars. They don't have to be painful ones, but they will be there. Each of you will carry the memories of what you've experienced and what you've endured for the rest of your life. And no amount of time, therapy or personal growth will change this. You are not the same people that you were. Regrettably, some couples re-launch their relation-ship without having fully considered that the crew members have changed and that means that they will be playing new roles that will impact them both. Failing to acknowledge this can result in more storms, hopefully none as big as the tidal wave, but unless you've each accepted the new roles you will be playing, your relation-ship will be more vulnerable to being capsized, even by the smallest squalls. Furthermore, it could seriously impede the journeys that you may want to take together.

In Chapter 6, we explored which elements of your relation-ship you wanted to save and which you know you will need to do more work on. In this chapter the focus is on each of you as crew members. What 'you' will need as an individual who is in recovery from addiction, and what 'you' will need as someone who is recovering from the trauma of discovery. We will also look at what it will be like for you as individuals to set sail again with your fellow crew mate.

In the next two chapters we will look at the role of forgiveness, how to rebuild trust and how to develop intimacy, but before you start that process, it's important that both of you have acknowledged the new roles that will form the foundation of your relationship together. We'll start by looking at what it means to be a partner of someone with sex or porn addiction who is surviving the trauma of betrayal, and what that means for the addicted partner. Then we will look at what it means to be the addicted partner in recovery from addiction and the impact that has on their partner.

Being a survivor of betrayal trauma

Every partner reacts differently to the discovery of sex or porn addiction. For a few, it's a relief to finally know what's going on and know that the difficulties they'd been experiencing for years in the relationship can finally be addressed and resolved. But for many, it is traumatising, and the journey to recovery is a long and emotionally draining one. How long that journey takes will depend on individual circumstances: how severe the addiction was, the level of deceit, the ability of the addicted partner to be honest and get into recovery, and the individual history and resources of the partner. But whatever the journey, it will be one that requires establishing personal safety and emotional stability, rebuilding self-esteem, avoiding triggers and learning to manage unavoidable ones, maintaining a support network, and resolving any underlying emotional or psychological issues that may have resurfaced due to the trauma.

You've probably made progress in many of these areas already, but unfortunately the nature of trauma is that you'll always be vulnerable to triggers that will remind you of what you've been through and may destabilise your emotional equilibrium. You may also continue to be sensitive to betrayals and dishonesty of any kind, from anyone, and hence your journey of recovery and personal growth will be ongoing. The good news, though, is that as you continue to heal and grow, you will also develop a level of resilience, confidence and compassion that you might hitherto have been unaware of. And these strengths will be ones you can take into every area of your life, and ones that will benefit all of your relationships. Below is a summary of what recovering from betrayal trauma looks like, and the impact that recovery may have on your addicted partner.

Recovering from trauma	Impact on addicted partner
Establishing personal safety – setting boundaries to keep yourself feeling safe and secure, around your addicted partner, but also in other areas of your life	For your partner to regain a sense of personal safety, they will need to set boundaries, and inevitably some of those will have a direct impact on you. This may include boundaries around where you go and what you do, both personally and as a couple. Over time, these boundaries will get easier, but initially you should expect to feel limited and will need to manage any feelings that you're 'being controlled', but rather remember this is a consequence of your addiction
Establishing emotional stability – like above, this often involves setting boundaries, but it will also mean learning to respond to situations in different ways, ways that are healthy for you and fit with your value system	Establishing emotional stability after trauma takes time. You should expect that there will continue to be emotional outbursts and unfair accusations while your partner learns to manage their emotions in a more constructive way. You will need to respond with patience and kindness, always remembering that this is a consequence of the trauma the addiction and deceit has caused
Rebuilding self-esteem – as well as positive self-affirmation, this will also mean taking time to focus on other areas of your life that give you pleasure and where you can get a true sense of your strengths and identity	Your partner will need to rebuild their self-esteem and that will mean you'll need to make a conscious effort to be reassuring and affirming. It also means your partner will need more time and space to pursue other areas of their life where they find affirmation
Avoiding triggers – there will be some situations that you know will be triggering and in the early stage of recovering from trauma it's wiser to avoid these situations until you feel more confident in your ability to manage them	Like someone in recovery, partners are triggered too, and where possible these trigger situations need to be avoided. This means there may be people, places and things your partner no longer wants to do, on their own, or as a couple. This is an area where you will need to develop a collaborative approach

Recovering from trauma	Impact on addicted partner
Managing unavoidable triggers – regrettably there will be some triggers you can't avoid, such as seeing a certain person, or type of person, or seeing something on the television. On these occasions you should have a list of strategies for establishing your sense of safety and stability again	There will be times when your partner will inadvertently be triggered, and when that happens, they're likely to behave irrationally. This is normal and natural when recovering from trauma and you will need to remain sensitive and learn to respond appropriately and discuss with your partner how to help them re-establish their equilibrium
Maintaining a support network – all partners benefit from having someone they can confide in. That may be a friend or family member or it may be within a community of other partners in recovery	You will need to ensure that your partner has sufficient time and space to get their own personal support, from whoever they believe is best to fulfil that role. Many people with addiction worry what is being said about them and can feel very uncomfortable that their story is being shared elsewhere. They often worry that their partner is not getting the 'right' support and sometimes seems worse after sharing with others. Remember this is your partner's responsibility to get the support they need in the way that works best for them
Resolving other emotional and psychological issues – for many partners this includes individual therapy, personal reading and sharing with others	Your partner will have their own history of issues that they may need to explore further and resolve. Your addiction didn't cause this, but it resurrected it. It's important to remember that this is 'their' time and it's up to them how much they want to share with you

Discovering your partner is addicted to sex or porn is not only traumatising, it's life-changing, but those life changes can provide many long-term benefits, regardless of what eventually happens to your relationship. Any trauma provides an opportunity for personal growth; it may not be one that you wanted, but nonetheless, it has happened and you have a choice about whether you face it full on and grow, or let it leave you floundering forever.

It's painful being an addicted partner of someone who is recovering from a trauma that 'you' caused. There can be acute feelings of shame as well as fear that the damage caused is irreparable. Sometimes you may find yourself getting defensive as a way of protecting your-self from the shame and fear, but if you truly want your partner to recover, you need to give them the space they need to do whatever they need to do. Some of that will be uncomfortable, but a successful relationship is based on two whole people, not two halves, so you need to provide the environment where they can fully heal.

Being in recovery from sex/porn addiction

Recovery is different for everyone, but there are some common factors that each of you need to be aware of. The first thing is that you will be 'in recovery' for the rest of your life, and that's a good thing, not a life sentence. What that means is that you will need to be aware that you have a vulnerability to addiction – not just sex and/or porn, but a susceptibility to developing other addictions, such as alcohol, work or exercise. You have a responsibility to make self-care a priority in your life, both emotionally and physically, and ensure that you avoid any known triggering behaviours or environments. In addition, you're also responsible for resolving any underlying issues, such as trauma and/or difficulties in childhood that may have led to negative self-beliefs or destructive behaviours. You will also need to continue regular recovery activities and stay in touch with a recovery community, whether that's 12-Step, aftercare groups or individual contact. The severity of your addiction will determine how often that needs to be and for how long.

Assuming you're actively working on your addiction, none of the above will be a surprise to you, but this is a lifetime commitment that will not only keep you safe from acting out, but it will save you the discomfort of 'white-knuckling' when you're triggered; crucially, it is also these activities that will demonstrate to your partner that you are truly 'in recovery', not simply abstaining. Below is a summary of what being in recovery looks like, and the impact it may have on partners.

Addiction recovery activities	Impact on partner
Emotional self-care – developing greater emotional awareness and setting appropriate boundaries to look after yourself and seeking emotional support from others	As your addicted partner develops greater emotional maturity they may become more assertive in asking for their emotional needs to be met, whether that's from you or by setting boundaries around wanting to spend more time alone, or with other friends and family or engaging in hobbies and other pastimes

Addiction recovery activities	Impact on partner
Physical self-care – including eating a healthy diet, developing a regular sleep routine and getting regular exercise. May also include regular activities such as mindfulness, meditation or yoga	Physical self-care is essential for recovery, which means your addicted partner's eating and sleeping routines may change. They may want to spend more time engaging in physical activities, whether that's going to a gym, playing sport or attending an exercise class
Avoid triggers – at least for the first two years of recovery you will need to avoid any people, places or things that you have identified as dangerous to your recovery	Any situations that might be triggering for an addicted partner in recovery should be avoided, at least until recovery is secure. Inevitably, this may put restrictions on you too. For example, there may be work opportunities that need to be missed, or places or social events and activities that you can't attend or enjoy together. This may also impact your sexual relationship if there are particular behaviours that need to be avoided – we'll look at that more in Chapter 14
Manage unavoidable triggers – regrettably there will be some triggers that you cannot avoid and in these situations you will need to use the relapse prevention strategies that you have learned during recovery	A hard fact for many partners to accept is that there will always be triggers. Over time these will subside, but regrettably because of the sexualised world that we live in, triggers can never be completely avoided. There may be times when your addicted partner seems to act irrationally, leaving an event early or suddenly wanting to change TV channel, or insisting on changing seat with you in a restaurant. This can be very upsetting for partners, but it is better for both of you that triggers are managed immediately. There's more on this in Chapter 13
Resolve underlying issues – unless you get to the root cause of your addiction, you will always be vulnerable to relapse. Individual therapy and personal reading and reflection are often the best ways to approach this	The majority of people in recovery need to work on resolving the underlying cause of the addiction. For many this involves individual therapy, which by its nature excludes the partner. This can leave some partners feeling rejected or betrayed as they wonder exactly what's being talked about. Where possible, it's good to share what's being learned in individual therapy, but remember it's a 'work in progress', and the addict's journey of individual discovery, and hence feedback, will be limited or inconsequential at times

Addiction recovery activities	Impact on partner
Staying in recovery community – maintaining regular contact with others in recovery, whether that's attendance at 12-Step, or aftercare or continuing individual contact with others in recovery is essential for accountability and a great benefit to personal growth	Partners often struggle with the confidentiality required for maintaining ongoing recovery support, but it is an essential resource for anyone in recovery. Your addicted partner will need time to attend meetings and make phone calls. They will also need complete privacy to make and take calls, or communicate via a messaging service. Understandably this can be triggering for partners, but it's not about the addicted partner being secretive, but about respecting the confidentiality of others and taking responsibility for their recovery

If the above seems arduous, it really isn't. The bottom line is that being in recovery from addiction means looking after yourself and taking responsibility for your emotional and physical well-being and happiness. It's about building a life where you no longer need, or want, any kind of unhealthy, compulsive behaviour.

As a partner of someone in recovery, it means you will be in a relationship with someone who is happy and whole, and emotionally available to fully share life with you. It can be difficult when you already feel so betrayed, and understandably view your addicted partner as acting selfishly throughout their active addiction, but in recovery, they will also need to be selfish, in as much as they need to prioritise whatever will keep them well. That can be tough, but remember – this is not for their benefit alone, but for both of you as a couple.

So as you have read, each of you will be taking up new roles. Rather than simply being two individuals in a relationship, one of you will also carry the role of being in recovery from addiction and the other the role of being a survivor of trauma. And each of you will have a further role, and that is being a supporter of the other's journey. The biggest blocks to accepting these new roles are shame and blame – we will look at each of these now.

Overcoming shame

We've already talked a lot about shame in this book, and recognised that it's an emotion that is often experienced by both the person with the addiction and their partner. We've seen how it can limit recovery from addiction and also trauma, but here we will focus on how it can impact developing an equal, collaborative relationship.

When an addicted partner is trapped in shame, they're unlikely to devote the time they require to their recovery because they feel they're not entitled to develop a whole and happy life. They may struggle with the self-focused attention they need to maintain their recovery, worrying that it's selfish and self-centred. Many find themselves in an almost permanent child-like state within the relationship, becoming compliant to whatever a partner wants, or indeed to whatever they assume their partner wants. Conversely, some respond to shame by becoming a defiant and defensive child, seeing every partner request or comment as an attack. In their desperate attempt to avoid feeling shame, they may find it impossible to tolerate their partner's needs for their trauma recovery, because it reminds them of the pain their behaviours have caused.

A partner who is trapped in shame may also find themselves taking a child-like role, feeling responsible for their addicted partner's recovery and failing to focus on their own. They can also become defensive, viewing any request from the addicted partner as a personal judgement on themselves. They may refuse to change and adapt because doing so may unconsciously reinforce their own fears that, at some level, the addiction occurred because there was something wrong with them.

According to Brene Brown, one of the world's leading experts on shame, perfectionism is at the root of shame (Brown, 2010). When we can view our faults and failings with compassion and recognise that being human means making mistakes, we can stop judging ourselves as not good enough, and instead, make peace with our vulnerability. That process has to happen from within, although compassionate sharing with others who experience the same emotions can also help enormously. If shame is something you're still struggling to overcome, the first step is to talk about it – whether that's within individual therapy or group work.

Ending the blame game

Blame is a natural response for anyone who's been hurt and the blame game can trap both partners and addicted partners. The blame game plays like this: I'm hurting, I want to know whose fault it is, so I find someone, or something to blame. In the short term, I feel better because I can tell myself that it's not my fault and hence I protect myself from shame and responsibility, but inadvertently what I'm also doing is saying that I am powerless to change anything. When we blame others for how we think, feel or behave, we give away our autonomy and our power to change our lives for the better. Over time, as the blame game continues and our sense of empowerment diminishes, we become increasingly vulnerable to being hurt by others.

Blame is also a tool for avoiding shame and is common in couples recovering from sex addiction (Collins & Collins, 2017). When we behave in a certain way that leaves us feeling shame, we may use blame as a strategy to avoid taking responsibility and make it our partner's fault. The consequence of this is not only disempowerment, but it also increases conflict and damages intimacy.

Blame is about deciding whose fault something is and it's often confused with responsibility, but it is absolutely not the same thing. If you are a partner of someone with an addiction, the addiction is most definitely 'their' responsibility. And if you're an addicted partner who is aware, for example, that your addiction arose from childhood abuse, then that abuse was the 'abuser's' responsibility. However, continuing to blame them will focus your attention on punishment, retribution and self-protection, rather than focusing on your ability to take control, heal and grow.

Ultimately, letting go of both shame and blame requires a process of acceptance and forgiveness – the latter we will look at in depth in Chapter 12. It takes time and effort, humility and courage, but if you want to be equal crew members on your new relation-ship, both of whom feel empowered to choose and navigate your future together, then both shame and blame need to be thrown overboard. There will undoubtedly be storms ahead, there are in every relationship, but when you steer your ship together, as equals, you can avoid the devastation you've experienced before.

The partnership contract below has been adapted from RecoveryNation.com. Take some time to read through it and see if this is something you can sign up to. If there are some points that jar with you, talk it through your therapist or someone you trust in recovery.

The Partnership Contract

Addicted partner

I, (name) _____ do pledge:

- To take personal responsibility for ending addiction in my life.
- To not allow any excuses, obstacles or challenges distract me from this responsibility.
- To make the transition to a healthy life a top priority – above even saving my marriage/relationship.
- To invest my time in developing new life management skills and learning how to effectively use them.
- To make decisions based on long-term health, not short-term advantage.
- To encourage my partner in their healing efforts. Not to hijack or manage those efforts, but to support their management of them.
- To not seek or assign blame for the problems in our relationship, but rather to acknowledge that there are problems and work together to solve them.
- To never consciously deceive my partner as a means of minimising personal responsibility for my actions or 'protecting' him/her from pain.
- To not allow a single compulsive urge to go unchallenged. I may not be able to control these urges, but I will never allow them to evolve into destructive action without putting up a conscious fight.
- To immediately share with my partner, support system and/or recovery coach any ritual that I do not manage successfully.
- To communicate to my partner and/or support system those times when I recognise complacency, confusion or conflict settling in to my recovery.

- To monitor my recovery for signs of 'going through the motions' and take action when such signs are observed.
- To seek as a privilege, not a punishment, opportunities to develop my emotional maturity and life skills.
- To learn and respect the evolving values of my partner.
- To accept all consequences of all my decisions. That includes any decision to withhold information, to engage in secret behaviour, etc. I understand that it doesn't matter if the consequences are reasonable or just. Just as I have chosen to engage in the behaviour, others have the choice of how they will respond. I am responsible for my actions.
- To accept all consequences from having violated my partner's boundaries. This, as dictated by my partner's observations, not my own.
- To keep mindful that my partner is imperfect and deserves understanding and patience. That they will make mistakes – some in direct contradiction to what is healthy.
- To discover, acknowledge and eliminate all destructive communication rituals that I engage in.
- To never use violence, emotional abuse, coercion or other threats to manipulate or otherwise control/repress my partner.
- To respect my partner's boundaries surrounding sexuality: including a refrain from unwanted sexual advances, sexual pressure, sexual expectation, etc. I recognise that any sexual activity between us during this period of recovery must be mutually desired.

Partner

I, (name) _____ do pledge:

- To take personal responsibility for healing from the trauma that I have experienced. I have both the right to heal and the right to live a healthy life.
- To surround myself with healthy people.
- To allow myself to feel the pain of this discovery without shame or embarrassment. I did not cause this addiction.

Our relationship did not cause this addiction. Both have merely been caught in its web.

- To understand that there is no path that I am 'supposed to' follow. That whatever I feel, is natural. When it becomes destructive to my own life or others (e.g. neglecting my kids, my career, my friends, etc.), it is my responsibility to take action. I am accountable for the destruction that results from my behaviour – even if that behaviour is directly related to my partner's addiction.

- To hold my addicted partner accountable as a mature adult, not a child. That their skills may be immature is not a sufficient reason to lesson my expectations of them acting like an adult. I will be compassionate as they develop this maturity, but will hold them accountable for what they do during the development.

- To share my feelings, thoughts and experiences openly – using healthy judgement as to when, to whom and how I share them.

- To rebuild trust in my instincts. To use these instincts in guiding the grey areas of my life. To develop the courage to act on these instincts.

- To separate my healing needs from my partner's recovery needs – acknowledging we have different paths to travel as individuals, but respecting the importance of both.

- To build a life of my own, capable of sustaining meaning and fulfilment regardless of my partner's commitment to their recovery.

- To acknowledge that challenges existed within our marriage/relationship prior to the discovery of this addiction.

- To not use avoidance as means of managing our relationship.

- To acknowledge that I have made mistakes in my own life, in our relationship and will continue to make mistakes.

- To not settle for sticking my head in the sand. I do not want to sweep this crisis under the rug, nor do I want it to just go away. Instead, I want to take the time we need to fundamentally change our relationship.

- To establish a boundary system that is clear and healthy; to teach my addicted partner those boundaries; and to work together to enforce them. This means providing ongoing feedback, support and encouragement to my addicted partner as they recognise those boundaries.
- To encourage and support my addicted partner in their effort to change their life.
- To understand that my partner will not achieve perfection in recovery. That they will make mistakes – some irrational, some selfish, some immature – that could serve as grounds for destroying any progress that has been made. I will instead place these actions in the context of addiction recovery, not perfection. Within reason, I will accept gradual progress in my partner's recovery when it is accompanied by sincere effort.
- To seek out changes in my addicted partner with objectivity and optimism. I want them to succeed. I want them to become healthy.
- To keep perspective between the ideals and the reality of my partner's recovery. For instance, while I would like them to experience no urges, I know this is an unrealistic ideal. In reality, I will separate these urges from their response to them.
- To provide my addicted partner with a safe environment from which they can learn about their addiction, pursue recovery and transition into a healthy person.

Recovery for couples is possible, and indeed, you can do more than survive, you can thrive. My experience of working with, and talking to, couples in recovery who are enjoying their new relation-ship has taught me the importance of the following 10 key principles.

1. They blame the addiction, not each other
2. They each accept responsibility for how they think, feel and behave
3. They each accept responsibility for meeting their own recovery needs and becoming happy and whole

4. They have support from others in their individual recovery
5. They support each other in their individual recovery
6. They empathise with each other
7. They respect each other
8. They're honest with each other
9. They give each other the benefit of the doubt
10. They commit to rebuilding trust and developing deeper intimacy

If you can adopt the above, or at least continue to work together to reach a place where you can, then you can rebuild your relation-ship and look forward to your life journey together. Before we move on to the critical issues of rebuilding trust and intimacy, I'd like to leave you with a few words from some of the survey participants.

> We're much more open, reflective, clean, honest, willing to risk conflict yet finding we rarely get into conflict, or it's very quickly resolved. We're more collaborative on everything. He's no longer 'the enemy'. (Partner)

> We are definitely closer now and my husband is a lot more open with me about if he is feeling stressed or triggered. It is generally a happier home for us, and the children, and we all make more time for each other. (Partner)

> I have the relationship I always wanted. (Addicted partner)

> It's so amazing to be free from all the secrets and lies and to still be loved and accepted. We have both realised that here were many things that needed to be worked through in our rela-tionship and having done that we are now closer than before. (Addicted partner)

References

Brown, B. (2010) *The Gifts of Imperfection, Let Go of Who You Think You're Supposed to Be and Embrace Who You Are.* Center City, MN: Hazelden Publishing.

Collins, P.C., Collins, G.N. (2017) *A Couples Guide to Sexual Addiction – A step-by-step plan to rebuild trust and restore intimacy.* New York: Adams Media.

Chapter 12

Understanding the essential role of forgiveness

In the last chapter we saw how forgiveness is essential for letting go of shame and blame and taking up your role as equal crew members on your new relation-ship. Forgiveness is also essential for beginning to rebuild trust and deepening intimacy, both of which we will look at in depth over the next two chapters. In this chapter we will focus on what forgiveness is, and what it isn't, the importance of forgiving your partner and yourself, the process of forgiveness and how to overcome blocks that may be getting in your way.

Put simply, forgiving is essential for overcoming addiction and trauma as individuals. Without it, you will lock yourselves in the past, weighted down with pain, anger, shame and regret. When you forgive, you begin the process of freeing yourselves from those painful emotions and give yourselves the chance to live again. In terms of your relationship, unforgiveness will keep you trapped in a cycle of shame and blame, distance and conflict. Using our boat metaphor, unforgiveness is like an old rope that ties you to the harbour, and unless you cast off, you will stay stuck in the same place forever. It may be tempting to think that being tied to the harbour is a safe place, but as the famous saying goes "ships may be safe in harbour, but that's not what they're built for".

How to move on

In *Getting Past the Affair* (Snyder et al., 2007), a book based on a scientifically evaluated treatment programme, seven steps are offered to recover, as a couple, from relationship trauma. Some of those steps have already been covered in previous chapters, but we will look at each of those steps now to see how forgiveness fits with the process.

1. *Recognition* – this is where the person with the addiction acknowledges the fact that they have an addiction and fully understands both the consequences of their addiction and they begin their recovery journey.

2. *Responsibility* – taking responsibility means working on your own recovery, whether from trauma or addiction, which we explored in depth in Chapter 3. For the addicted partner, it means taking full responsibility for the choices they made in the past and the choices they make in the future.

3. *Remorse* – the addicted partner needs to express genuine remorse and be able to empathise with the hurt, pain and trauma they have caused their partner. The emotional restitution letter described in Chapter 7 provides an opportunity to do this. Demonstrating remorse is crucial if you want the relationship to move on, and it is a key ingredient in forgiveness.

4. *Restitution* – this step is where the addicted partner actively engages in positive actions to minimise harm and put things right. For those in 12-Step, this is where you are making active amends. Without self-forgiveness, restitution may come from a place of shame and guilt, rather than from genuine empathy and care.

5. *Reform* – we talked a lot about the importance of demonstrating commitment to change in the last chapter. This is going to include your couple contract and also the accountability contract. Demonstrating reform allows partners to consider forgiving the past, rather than getting trapped in requiring ongoing restitution.

6. *Release* – this is the step where forgiveness plays a critical role. It is where the betrayed partner commits to letting go of the pain, hurt and anger and makes a positive choice to give up their right to continue reminding the addicted partner of what they've done, favouring instead to focus on what they're doing now and what they want in the future.

7. *Reconciliation* – reconciling means building an equal relationship again, one where there is complete honesty and intimacy. How that can be achieved is covered in the next two chapters.

As you can see from the above, forgiveness is critical for the final reconciliation stage of moving on to occur and the previous steps all pave the way to make forgiveness possible. If you feel you have missed any of these steps, go back to the relevant chapters and see what further work needs to be done.

What forgiveness means

Forgiveness is something that people often don't talk about and when they do, it's often shrouded in religious connotations. More commonly we refer to the principles of forgiveness in language such as 'letting go', or perhaps 'coming to terms with'. What language you prefer doesn't really matter, what matters is that both of you know what you mean when you're talking about 'forgiving'.

Forgiveness is often confused with excusing, or pardoning or letting someone off, but that's not what it means and without a clear understanding it can be difficult to understand why you'd ever want to forgive. Forgiveness doesn't mean that the wrong doesn't matter anymore, nor does it mean that everything is going to be all right between you in the future. And forgiving, definitely doesn't mean forgetting. It's not excusing someone or condoning something that's wrong. It doesn't mean that you're willing to tolerate something that's unacceptable to you and it doesn't let anyone off from the consequences of what they've done. Forgiveness is not a pardon, nor does it reduce the sentence: the price still has to be paid. Forgiving also doesn't mean that you won't still feel pain, or that you don't have to talk about it anymore. Regrettably, forgiveness also doesn't automatically protect you from making the same mistake again, or of being hurt again.

First and foremost, forgiveness is a conscious choice. You do not 'have' to forgive yourself, or your partner. Forgiveness is a process, not a single, discrete event; it takes time. Hence, making a decision to forgive means that you've started the process, not finished it. Forgiveness means releasing yourself and your partner from further punishment and freeing yourself from the hurt, anger and shame that past behaviours have caused.

What helps the forgiveness process

We learn about forgiveness throughout our lives, right from the earliest time you saw a parent or sibling do something wrong, or indeed when you did something wrong. We will all have experiences of when we have hurt other people, whether that was deliberate or not. And we will all have experiences of being hurt by others, sometimes accidentally, sometimes intentionally. Your personal experience of forgiveness will influence how you approach the challenge of forgiving yourself and forgiving your partner. Take some time now to reflect on what you have learned about forgiveness throughout your life. What have been your personal experiences of forgiving yourself? Forgiving someone else? Being forgiven? What have been the benefits and consequences of that?

Looking back at our past can also help us to recognise the role of compassion in forgiveness. Whether we are forgiving ourselves, or someone else, we need to be able to recognise that part of being human means that we're not perfect and sometimes we make mistakes that hurt other people as well as ourselves. I doubt there is a person on the planet that can't look back at their life and see things they regret and wish they'd done differently. And it's our individual choice whether we live with those regrets by constantly chastising ourselves, or the other, or if we see ourselves and others with compassion and let it go.

For the person who is hoping to receive forgiveness, the best way to help that process is to stop doing things that are hurtful and actively engage in behaviours that demonstrate you have changed. This may sound very obvious, and indeed it is, but many couples become resentful that they have not yet been forgiven, but continue to behave in ways that are thoughtless and uncaring. The more you can do to show that the hurtful behaviours really are in the past, the easier it will be for your partner to leave them there.

For any change to happen, we need to have sufficient motivation to make the change, and when we're talking about the difficult process of forgiveness, holding in mind the future you want to have will be a great motivator. Your vision should include who you want to be as a person; someone who is compassionate and caring, rather than bitter and resentful; someone who is not plagued with guilt and shame. Remember also the vision you want for your relationship, one that is mutually respectful and loving; one where trust can be rebuilt and intimacy deepened.

Blocks to forgiveness

There are a number of reasons why couples recovering from sex and porn addiction can find it particularly difficult to forgive, both themselves and each other. The blocks to forgiveness below have been separated into those most common to partners and those most common to the person with the addiction.

For partners

Wanting safety – many partners fear that if they stop hurting and start to 'act normal' their addicted partner will give up on their recovery and act out again. Some partners also struggle to forgive themselves for not knowing what was going on and fear that if they let go of the pain, they'll leave themselves vulnerable to being hurt again. Not forgiving stems from insecurity, but in reality, not letting go fuels insecurity, because it means that your damaged emotions never have the chance to heal. By forgiving you become strong again, you can begin to let go of the constant vigilance and direct your energies into developing the relationship that you want and deserve.

Wanting justice – what happened wasn't fair; you are the innocent victim of your addicted partner's decisions and behaviour. However, refusing to forgive will not change that fact. The greater injustice will not be forgiving your addicted partner, but choosing not to free yourself from the pain of the past.

Wanting control – rebuilding trust is a fragile process, as we will see in the next chapter, and it's tempting to continue to show how hurt you are to try and get your addicted partner's undivided attention and to unquestioningly comply with your needs. But this will not build trust because you'll never be sure if their behaviour change is in response to your emotions or because they have fundamentally changed.

Wanting the moral high ground – this block has its roots in the belief that forgiving is equivalent to saying the crime was acceptable and refusing forgiveness allows them to demonstrate how strongly the behaviour opposed their value system. Partners who struggle with this are often struggling with low self-esteem and need to prove that they are better than the addicted partner. Unfortunately, all it does is tie the partner to the position of martyr, rather than survivor.

The addicted partner

Wanting to feel bad – this may seem crazy, and indeed it is, but many addicted partners don't want to forgive themselves because they feel they don't deserve to feel better about themselves. This block is rooted in ongoing shame that not only hinders the addicted partner's recovery, but also damages developing an equal loving relationship.

Wanting sobriety – some believe that staying in shame will help them not to relapse. They fear that forgiving themselves might mean they forget the damage the addiction has caused. However, failing to forgive yourself is not an effective relapse prevention strategy. In fact, it can be quite the opposite, as it keeps you trapped in shame and negative emotions that are more likely to cause a relapse.

Wanting sympathy – some addicted partners don't want to forgive themselves because they think that all the time they continue to live with the shame, their partner will feel sorry for them and will be more likely to be compassionate and forgiving. In reality, the 'down dog' position soon becomes tiring for partners and it's more likely to be viewed as weakness than humility and remorse.

Wanting security – some addicted partners continue to hold resentments at the way their partner reacted to discovering the addiction. It's common for partners to say and do things in the midst of trauma that can be hurtful to the person who hurt them; they may also do things that hurt other people, such as disclosing the behaviour to others, who on reflection didn't need to know. Not forgiving may seem to protect you from this behaviour as you tell yourself that now you know what your partner is capable of, but in reality it will just get in the way of developing the relationship you want to have and hinder your partner's recovery from trauma.

Overcoming blocks to forgiveness

If you know that you're struggling with some of the blocks identified above, then the following exercise can help you begin to move forward. The exercise below is based on one that is commonly used in both CBT (cognitive behavioural therapy) and in motivational interviewing. It involves listing the risks and benefits of letting go of your feelings of hurt, anger and regret, and then listing the risks and benefits of not letting go. It might look something like the example below.

	Risks	Benefits
Letting go	I'll get hurt again I'll forget the consequences of what happened My partner will forget how much they've hurt me My partner will think what they did doesn't matter anymore My partner will think I've forgotten how much I hurt them I/my partner will act out again My partner will have 'gotten away with it'	I'll stop going over the details of the past I'll be able to focus on my future, rather than my past I'll have more energy for my recovery As a couple we can focus on the positives that we're building I can stop feeling angry and bitter I can stop feeling shame and regret As a couple we'll be more able to enjoy time together
Not letting go	I will stay angry forever We will argue I'll continually think about what happened in the past I won't be able to move forward We won't develop an equal relationship I won't be able to notice or celebrate the positive changes in our relationship	My partner will never forget what they did to me I'll protect myself from getting hurt again My partner will feel sorry for me My partner will continue to feel guilt and shame

As you complete this exercise you'll begin to notice that the benefits of letting go significantly outweigh the benefits of not letting go. Hopefully that knowledge will help you to recognise that if you want your relationship to be a happy and loving one, forgiveness is essential. Knowing this is a great start, but remember – the journey of forgiveness is a long one, and one that you will need to do in your own time. Below are some thoughts on what some of your first steps might be.

How to start the forgiveness journey

The more you're able to develop compassion for yourself and your partner, the easier it will be to begin the forgiveness journey. If you've worked through the previous exercises in this book, you'll both be aware of the reasons why the addiction developed. It's important to understand that these reasons are explanations, not excuses or justifications. When both of you are able to understand how the addiction developed with compassion, it's easier to begin to let go of the consequences. For example, when you can honestly say 'I understand that this addiction developed because you came from a broken home, with little love and affection, where you were made to feel shame about needing attention and that's why you found it difficult to be vulnerable with me and instead turned to acting out behaviours', then you begin to move forward. It doesn't excuse the choices that were made, but it helps to provide a perspective of understanding and compassion. For partners, it further helps them to see that the acting out was not a deliberate attempt to hurt them, but a failed attempt by the addicted partner to recover from childhood wounds.

If you feel ready to start the process of forgiveness, then the next step is to break down what's happened into smaller chunks. Forgiving everything will understandably feel like an overwhelming task, but if you break the task down, you'll find that some elements are easier to forgive than others. Indeed, you'll probably notice that some of the forgiveness journey has already been made. With regard to acting-out behaviours, you may find it much easier to forgive, for example, watching pornography, but harder to forgive seeing sex workers. When it comes to the deceit and lies, it may be easier to let go of the acting out behaviours that happened when your addicted partner was away on business than the ones that happened while at home. You may also find it easier to forgive behaviours that happened before the relationship started, or ones that occurred during particularly heavy times of stress. Every couple's story is different, which means every couple's journey of forgiveness is also different.

Beginning to forgive is in part an act of will and discipline. Once you've made a decision to forgive something, you need to redirect your attention from thinking about it, especially dwelling on the details and the hurt and pain you feel. Each time you re-live an event, you'll keep the pain alive, but when you can redirect your thoughts to the changes that you've seen and the hopes you have for the future, the power of the past will diminish. In forgiveness, you'll find freedom – but remember, it's a journey that will take time.

To summarise, forgiveness doesn't mean forgetting or saying it didn't matter, it means letting go of painful emotions and looking ahead rather than back. It takes time and sometimes you'll feel like you're moving forward and then find yourself back at square one. However, with persistence you can leave your pain and regret in the past and focus on your future. You may always bear the scars, but you don't have to live with gaping wounds.

Reference

Snyder, D.K., Baucom, D.H., Gordon, K.C. (2007) *Getting Past the Affair: A program to help you cope, heal and move on – together or apart.* New York: The Guildford Press.

Chapter 13

Rebuilding trust

In Chapter 1 we looked at the fact that healthy relationships are built on trust and how sex addiction not only profoundly damages it, but often obliterates it. Regrettably, making a decision to re-commit to each other does not automatically mean trust returns; indeed, it can make it harder, as there is so much more to lose if trust is broken again.

Using our boat metaphor, trust is the hull. It is the basis on which the rest of your relation-ship is built and it is the single element that determines whether your relation-ship will float or sink. The stronger the hull, the better your relation-ship will fare in the storms of life. In this chapter we will focus on the process of rebuilding trust, not only within the relationship, but also the importance of learning to trust ourselves, but first we'll explore why people tell lies and deceive in the first place.

Why we lie

There are lots of reasons why people lie, and while it's convenient to say that only 'bad' people lie, that's simply not the truth. We all tell lies at times. Sometimes it's to protect ourselves, sometimes it's to protect others and when we feel our lies are justified we tend to refer to them as 'white lies'. However, lies damage not only trust, but intimacy as well, because they build walls of secrecy between people and stop the true self being known. Nonetheless, the truth can also hurt, and so on some occasions we withhold the full story or our real thoughts and feelings out of sensitivity. There are also different kinds of lies. Lies of omission – in other words, not telling because no one asked – and lies of commission when we deliberately say something that isn't true.

People with addiction generally lie out of fear and often it has become a habit that is hard to break. They may have learnt to lie in early childhood to protect themselves from consequences or to protect a parent or the family unit. Fear is often at the root of dishonesty. For the addicted partner, it could be fear of having to stop the behaviour if it was known, fear of losing a loved one, or children, or friends, or financial stability, or their reputation, or indeed all of these things. People with addictions also lie to protect themselves from the pain of not living up to someone else's expectations – or their own. They are often also desperately afraid of causing even more pain to an already traumatised partner. Hence, telling the truth can feel terrifying.

Partners can also develop a habit of telling lies; indeed, many only discovered the truth of the addiction as a result of their secretive investigations and clever verbal tricks. Some partners also struggle with shame around their need for reassurance and subsequently hide their checking-up behaviours and manipulate conversations rather than being direct.

There's another reason why many people lie and that is to protect their sense of autonomy. This is especially true for people who came from a family background where they were robbed of any privacy or not allowed to grow up and become a separate individual. All children tell lies and have secrets and this trait often becomes stronger in adolescence. As a child begins to form their own identity they need to keep things to themselves and if they're not given space to do that they will develop a secret life, rather than a separate one. Some adults continue to use lying as a strategy for having autonomy in relationships and those needs for autonomy and separateness are greater for some than others.

All couples will have different boundaries around what they perceive as secret and private. Some will have a 24/7 open-door policy – including the toilet door; they open each other's post, share frankly about their sexual histories and fantasies and discuss the intricacies of every conversation they have with other people. Others consider these things private and would feel embarrassed and offended if someone expected to talk to them while they were on the loo and affronted if they were not expected to maintain a friend's confidentiality. There's no right and wrong, just different, but when there has been a betrayal, the lines are much more blurred. Developing a broader understanding of the conscious and unconscious motivations for why we lie can help couples rebuild trust and provide an avenue for offering reassurance that honesty really is the best policy.

Evaluating trust in your relationship

We learn to trust from the day we are born. During our earliest years we trust our primary care givers to anticipate and meet our needs and as we grow towards adolescence, we learn to articulate our needs, trusting that they'll be met. Teenage and early adulthood is a time when we hopefully discover the art of negotiation and compromise, with caregivers and with partners and friends, trusting that our needs will be heard and respected, even if we don't always get what we want. If any of these developmental stages of trust building are disrupted, or indeed absent, we're more likely to become adults who struggle to trust others and instead become reliant on meeting our own needs.

Addiction often has its roots in disrupted early trust relationships, hence people with addiction learn to meet their own needs through their acting out, rather than trusting others to meet them; and as we've stated before, infidelity wrecks trust. Therefore, trust is often a problem for both partners recovering from sex and porn addiction. It's common to hear partners saying 'I can't trust you' and often, 'I want to trust you, but I can't'. In *Helping Couples Get Past the Affair*, Baucom describes the 'spreading effect' of violated trust (Baucom et al., 2011, p. 321). When trust in a partner has been lost through infidelity, it spreads to other domains of the relationship, leaving partners believing they can't trust their addicted partner in any way.

One of the most effective ways of beginning the journey of rebuilding trust is to identify the domains of the relationship where trust is intact and the areas where trust can most quickly and easily be developed. For example, someone may be trusted to be punctual, or to look after children or earn a living, but there may be areas where they are less reliable, such as remembering to pay bills, buy groceries or undertake chores thoroughly. Emphasis can then be made in the weaker areas by becoming more reliable in those. By acknowledging the relationship domains where trust is already present and paying attention to areas where simple changes can rebuild trust, a greater sense of trustworthiness can be developed. Trust also extends to the emotional realm, such as being able to trust your partner will empathise with you if you talk about a difficult day, or that they'll listen to your thoughts and feelings without judgements. This is another area where trust can quickly be rebuilt by adopting healthy communication skills. Take a look at the list of possible domains below and each of you mark where you feel are.

Domain	Completely trust	Trust a little	Don't trust at all
Being on time			
Sharing diary arrangements			
Sticking to practical commitments			
Looking after children			
Listening to children			
Household chores			
Earning money			
Managing money			
Being polite and courteous with family and friends			
Listening respectfully			

Once complete, celebrate the areas where you can already trust each other and then look at the middle column to see what you can practically do to rebuild trust in these areas. Once you've worked through that column, look at the domains where you don't trust at all and discuss what needs to change here. You'll see that this list does not include anything about relationship fidelity – that is what we come on to now.

Learning to trust yourself

Before you can begin to trust someone else, you need to learn to trust yourself. Addiction not only damages trust between partners, but also our ability to trust ourselves. Discovering deceit and betrayal often leaves partners feeling unable to trust their own judgements and in early recovery, addicted partners often doubt their ability to manage their negative emotions in healthy ways. This means that while both partners are desperately trying to rebuild trust with each other, they may internally doubt their own ability to do so.

In the same way as trusting others, our ability to trust ourselves comes from previous early experiences. If you were brought up in an environment where you were told you had no self-control, or you couldn't make decisions for yourself, or that you were always wrong in one way or another, then self-doubt may have become a pattern for you. But in the same way as there are domains of trust within a relationship, as explored in the previous section, there are also domains of trust within ourselves. Have another look at the table above and tick the areas where you already trust yourself and those areas where you can make simple improvements. As you gain more and more positive experiences of trusting yourself, your sense of internal trust will build.

Common myths about building trust

In the excellent book, *Worthy of Her Trust* (Arterburn & Martinkus, 2014), the following three common myths of trust building are explored.

Myth 1 – time heals all wounds and builds trust

No amount of time will heal the pain of betrayal. It's true that over time we do begin to forget what we've suffered, or at least, we forget the details, but as we've already explored, the world is full of triggers that can bring the memories crashing back. Assuming things will get better in time is a way of avoiding taking responsibility for the work involved in rebuilding trust. It also means you're making yourself powerless to speed up the process. Unfortunately, there are no fast-track ways to rebuild trust. No one moves from 'I don't trust you' to 'I do trust you' without passing through painful phases of partial trust and then crushing doubt. But there's no point, and no need, to leave it to a calendar – rebuilding trust is an active process, not a passive passing of time.

Myth 2 – not acting out again is all it takes to rebuild trust

Not acting out is undoubtedly essential to rebuilding trust, but because you'll never be able to prove a negative, there has to be much, much more than this. Furthermore, trust hasn't simply been broken around behaviours, but around the emotional bond between you as a couple. Partners no longer trust that they're loved and respected; hence, they need committed effort to rebuild trust in these areas. That means demonstrating care and commitment on a daily basis as well as becoming trustworthy in every other area of life. You can read more about what the true evidence of recovery is at the end of this chapter.

Myth 3 – trust will be restored when my partner stops being so controlling

It's often the person with the addiction who complains about being controlled, stating that it's impossible to build trust if every movement they make is being monitored. Similarly, some partners struggle to let go of control in order to let trust grow. However, it's important to understand that many partners' continuing efforts to control come from deep insecurities that have developed over many years of doubt and suspicion. Letting go of control goes hand-in-hand with rebuilding trust, as the addicted partner becomes increasingly trustworthy and the partner takes increasing risks. And remember, there's a significant difference between control and accountability; more on that later in this chapter.

The essential ingredients of trust

There are three essential ingredients of trust, all are equally important and each intertwines and depends on the other. Honesty cannot exist without some level of open accountability. For example, how can I trust you when you say you have bought milk if you won't let me open the refrigerator? Empathy is also essential: without empathy accountability feels like control, and honesty feels begrudged – both become reluctant rather than loving and open. And if empathy isn't accompanied by honesty and accountability, then it simply isn't empathy at all. Saying you understand means nothing if it's not backed up by both the spirit and the actions to support it. We will look at honesty, empathy and accountability in more depth now.

Honesty

For trust to be rebuilt, the person with the addiction needs to commit to honesty. Honesty about what's happened in the past, what's happening in the current moment and honesty in future commitments. Partners also need to be honest about their feelings and their failings, helping the addicted partner to understand their cycle of reaction and hence help to encourage and support them when they're feeling triggered. Both partners need to become honest about their needs, both their needs in recovery and their needs from each other.

Honesty needs to go far beyond the acting out behaviours. It should be assumed that acting out behaviours will or have stopped – that needs to be a prerequisite to rebuilding trust. Beyond that, there needs to be a general spirit of openness and transparency about everything. That means being honest if something has been forgotten or a mistake has been made. Being real about feelings and talking about difficulties and problems rather than pretending they don't exist. On the surface this may sound very appealing to partners, but complete honesty and openness will mean being ready to hear things that might be challenging or painful too.

Empathy

Most people are instinctively good at picking up on other people's emotions, but unfortunately some people often aren't very good at showing it. Empathy is all about letting your partner know that you understand not just what they said, but how they feel. It's hard to rebuild trust if you don't believe that your partner knows what you're feeling. After all, how can a partner trust an addicted partner's promise not to betray if the addicted partner can't communicate that they fully understand how much the previous betrayal hurt? And when a partner can empathise with the pain the addicted partner has experienced as a result of their addiction, they are more likely to trust that they don't want to act out again.

Fortunately, showing empathy is a skill that can be learnt by developing good listening skills and taking the time to consider how you would feel if you were in your partner's shoes. Empathy requires vulnerability and courage, because we don't want to feel the pain of someone else. Unlike sympathy that says 'that sounds painful for you', empathy says 'I can imagine what that pain feels like for you'. It's uncomfortable, but it's essential for rebuilding trust and intimacy. Empathy breaks through feelings of isolation and alienation and helps couples to experience both the highs and lows of emotion together.

Accountability

As we saw in Chapter 4, accountability provides protection for both partners. For the addicted partner it protects them not only from opportunities to act out, but also from being wrongly accused. It also protects them from witnessing the pain of insecurity that can dominate partners' lives. For partners, accountability can provide evidence that the addicted partner is committed to recovery, as well as security that they are where they say they are and doing what they say they are doing. We also looked at the importance of creating an accountability contract together. A document that is mutually agreed and one where both of you take responsibility for maintaining it. Working towards equality in every aspect of the relationship is one of the keys to rebuilding trust (Gottman, 2012).

As recovery becomes more established for both of you, your accountability contract will change and increasingly become a natural way that you keep in touch and manage your life. As you each become more aware of your triggers in individual recovery, these potential flashpoints should be worked into your contract. For example, if beach holidays are a trigger for both, or either of you, but it's something you want to do, then you'll need to work out how you can keep safe and offer reassurance in this situation. Similarly, if business travel is a trigger and perhaps something you've managed to avoid during the early months of recovery, you will need to create a strategy for managing this if your work life evolves.

To rebuild trust, accountability needs to become natural and routine; it's an opportunity to demonstrate reliability and commitment and reduce anxiety and conflict. If either of you is struggling with feelings of being controlled, or controlling, then it's also an opportunity to empathise and encourage each other that this is for the benefit of you as a couple, not just as individuals.

Using polygraphs

Some couples find it beneficial to make use of regular polygraph tests, sometimes referred to as lie-detector tests. Technically speaking, modern polygraphs do not measure lies, but rather assess the likely credibility of what someone is saying (Palmatier & Rovner, 2015). They do not provide a pass or fail result, but rather a percentage likelihood that what's been told has been true. One way to use polygraphs is to undertake a test following a therapeutic disclosure and then arrange six-monthly follow-ups to ask if there has been any acting out since the last polygraph.

Opinions on the use of polygraphs for building trust are mixed, with some feeling they are critical and others believing they are detrimental. In my experience, what rebuilds trust more than actually taking a polygraph test is the willingness to do so. If someone flatly refuses to undertake a test, then it's reasonable to wonder why.

Becoming trustworthy – advice for the addicted partner

If you want to rebuild your partner's trust, then you need to prove that you are trustworthy. In a nutshell, that means becoming 100 per cent transparent in everything you say and do and always following through with any commitment you make, however small. It also means learning to be proactive rather than reactive and pre-empting any potentially triggering situation for your partner, rather than waiting to be asked. In *Worthy of Her Trust*, Arterburn and Martinkus recommend adopting the following mantra: 'I would rather lose you, than lie to you' (Arterburn & Martinkus, 2014).

When you are able to adopt this mantra, you will be able to demonstrate that your highest priority in the relationship is not protecting yourself, but being trustworthy.

Some of what follows has already been covered in the accountability section in Chapter 4, but it is repeated here in case you've jumped to this section. Perhaps more importantly, the advice below is equally as important as your relationship moves on as it is when you're in the crisis stage.

Pro-active honesty – during your active addiction you will have spent much of your time hiding the truth from your partner and only being honest on an essential 'need to know basis', or when you knew you would be found out. From now on, proactive honesty needs to become an automatic way of living and being. In practice, this means ensuring you talk about where you're going, not where you've been, who you're seeing, not who you saw and what you're going to do, rather than what you've already done. It means you're the one who initiates looking through phone logs, bank statements, or software accountability reports. This is especially important if there is a potential trigger situation on the horizon. For example, if you are going to be away on business, you say 'I have a meeting next Tuesday and I will be away on Monday evening. There will be four people at the meeting, including a woman called Sally from the accounts department. I will be home by teatime'.

Be accurate – speaking in vague terms can be very triggering for partners and can inadvertently remind them of times when you didn't share the whole truth. From now on you need to be accurate and precise, no estimates, no approximately, no roughly. For example, picking up on the scenario above, you would say 'I have a meeting next Tuesday at 9.00 am at the central office in Salisbury. I will stay in the Salisbury Novotel on Monday night. The meeting will be with John, Peter and a woman called Sally from accounts, and the Chairman will join the meeting at 11.30. I will drive straight home after the meeting finishes at 2.00 and will be home by 4.30'.

T-30 Journal – The T-30 is an excellent trust-building strategy explained fully in *Worthy of Her Trust* (Arterburn & Martinkus, 2014). It is a simple spreadsheet that details your movements and allows you to account for your time. This strategy is especially helpful for situations such as being away from home. Following our example above, it might look like this:

8.00 pm	Leave home and drive to Salisbury Novotel
8.30 pm	Driving
9.00 pm	Driving
9.30 pm	Watch TV in my hotel room
10.00 pm	Watching TV
10.30 pm	Get ready for bed, read
11.00 pm	Sleep
7.00 am	Get up, shower, get dressed
7.30 am	Breakfast in hotel
8.00 am	Drive to meeting
8.30 am	Meeting at central office in Salisbury with Pete, John and Sally
9.00 am	Meeting as above
9.30 am	Meeting as above
10.00 am	Meeting as above
10.30 am	Coffee with Pete, John and Sally in office canteen
11.00 am	Chairman joins Pete, John, Sally and myself for meeting
11.30 am	Meeting as above
12.00 noon	Meeting as above
12.30 pm	Meeting as above
1.00 pm	Lunch with Chairman, John, Pete and Sally
1.30 pm	Lunch as above
2.00 pm	Final debrief meeting with John, Pete and Sally
2.30 pm	Drive home
3.00 pm	Drive home
3.30 pm	Drive home
4.00 pm	Arrive home, unpack

Once you've set up the template, this can then be quickly completed whenever required.

Technology transparency and tools – Although technology has often been a cause of many of your problems, it can also be a huge benefit in rebuilding trust. You should, of course, ensure that you have installed porn blockers and accountability software on all devices and no device should be used, outside of the office, in a situation where your partner can't clearly see what you're doing. You should also ensure that all passwords are shared and devices are always left face-up so notifications that come in can be seen. You can also set up GPS tracking on your devices so your partner knows, for example, that you are at the meeting in Salisbury and use video call to show that you are in your hotel bedroom and that you are in the meeting with the people you say you are with.

The 10-minute rule – this strategy is one recommended by Robert Weiss in his book *Out of the Doghouse* (Weiss, 2017). Have an agreement that if your partner telephones you and you're unable to answer the phone immediately, you will call back within 10 minutes. During that time, your partner agrees to give you the benefit of the doubt. Ten minutes should give you ample time to make an excuse to step out of a meeting for an 'emergency family situation', or to get to a safe place to return a call if you're driving. If you are in situations where you know you won't have phone access, for example on a plane or the underground, or if you know you definitely can't answer a call because of a particular meeting you have, then this can be marked on your T-30 journal.

Financial openness – if your acting out behaviour has included any financial transactions, then you need to ensure you have 100 per cent financial transparency. Obviously that means no private bank accounts or credit cards, but it also means open access to all bank and credit card statements. You should also agree a place to put receipts for any cash withdrawals and all purchases.

No surprises – finally, while trust is being rebuilt, do not, under any circumstances, plan to surprise your partner, even if your intentions are admirable ones. I remember a client sharing how he had decided to surprise his wife with a weekend break for her birthday. He had carefully made all the necessary arrangements for children to be looked after and bought special gifts to surprise her with when they arrived. The whole event went catastrophically wrong when she was thrown back into her trauma as realised she had no idea what he had been doing behind her back. If there is a birthday or anniversary coming up, check with your partner first how they want to celebrate. Not only are events like this often triggering in the first place, but any attempt at a surprise could seriously backfire.

Regrettably, there will be times when all the advice above fails, or indeed, times when you fail to use the advice above. If for any reason you have not lived up to your commitments in any way, if you've not been honest about something, or if you've had a slip of any kind, then the technique below can be used. You would be wise as a couple to have agreed this in advance, hoping it won't happen, but prepared if it does.

24-hour disclosure rule – if you have had a slip, not been 100 per cent honest about anything, or failed, or forgotten, do something you'd agreed to do, you have 24 hours to tell the truth. In these circumstances you cannot expect that your partner will not be angry or upset, or indeed that you won't have put your trust-building efforts back a step, but it sets a precedent that if you fail, or make a mistake, you will have the courage and integrity to own up to it.

In our Understanding Partners' Needs and Rebuilding Trust workshops, we often hear the struggles and complaints of addicted partners who feel they have been 'wrongly accused' – in 90 per cent of these situations, the 'accusation' could have been avoided completely if they had undertaken the advice above. However, the above is not a guarantee that there won't be times when your partner is suspicious and questions you or accuses you unfairly, and when that happens, your response needs to be one of patience and empathy. Becoming trustworthy will initially take a lot of conscious effort and at first it may feel exhausting, but over time, it will become increasingly automatic and simply be the way you operate your lives together.

Learning to take risks – advice for partners

The only way that trust can be tested is by taking risks. Without doubt and uncertainty, there would be no need for trust, hence building trust requires becoming more comfortable with our fears and managing the anxiety that taking risks will inevitably create.

In the early days, when trust is still very fragile, those risks will be small ones. Pushing yourself too soon could put you back, but conversely, if you always stay within your comfort zone, you'll never move forward. A good way of knowing when you're ready to take an extra risk is when the accountability contract is beginning to feel intrusive or upsetting. For example, if your addicted partner calling you every lunchtime is serving more of a reminder than a reassurance, then it might be time to move to a text message instead. Or if the agreement that your addicted partner never goes away on business without you is becoming a burden, then perhaps you can agree to risking a single overnight stay.

Taking risks is not about changing your non-negotiable boundaries. As Vicki Tidwell Palmer states, "boundaries aren't about something you do to another person. Boundaries are something you do for your own self-care, well-being, and protection" (Tidwell Palmer, 2016).

Over time you will notice your addicted partner is becoming more and more trustworthy, which means you will begin to feel safer and not need protection in as many areas of your relationship as you did. So, for example, an early boundary may have been that your addicted partner comes to bed at the same time as you, but you may feel increasingly comfortable that they really are just staying up late to watch the news.

The process of taking risks will naturally develop over time and it's important that you don't feel rushed or pressurised into doing something that will cause you significant anxiety. But remember, trust, by its very definition, is different from certainty. It requires acting on faith without being sure what the outcome will be.

Managing slips and relapse

Not everyone with an addiction has relapses, but it's not uncommon for there to be 'slips' (sometimes translated as Short Lapse In Progress) and regrettably some do go through periods of relapse while on the road to recovery. Acknowledging the reality of this and how the two of you will manage it is essential to the trust-building process. Evidence shows that when addicted partners confess their relapses, rather than waiting for it to be discovered or disclosed later, their relationships are stronger (Corley et al., 2012). What's more, the majority of partners suspected a relapse, and many who weren't told went on to discover for themselves, which then had a severe detrimental effect on building trust.

Each couple must decide for themselves what distinguishes a slip from a relapse and agree what will be disclosed. It is not beneficial to share every time there is a temptation as this will simply increase insecurity for partners, but if there is any kind of follow-through that leads to acting out, then disclosure will be required. However, you may agree between you that switching on the computer and Googling lingerie for a few minutes is a slip and need not be disclosed as long as it's discussed in therapy or a recovery group. Similarly, walking into a massage parlour but immediately leaving may also not be something that needs to be disclosed, as long as it's shared and addressed somewhere. Most couples agree that if slips become regular, or indeed lead on to an extended period of acting out, or any physical sexual encounter, then this is a relapse and should be disclosed. Below are some guidelines for how you as a couple can manage slips and relapses.

Guidelines for managing slips and relapses

- First and foremost, agree between you what constitutes a slip and what is a relapse. If this is difficult to do, then discuss with your individual counsellor and support network as well as with a couple counsellor.
- Agree what behaviours will be disclosed between you as a couple.
- In situations where you agree that a slip doesn't need to be disclosed between you, agree who this information needs to be shared with.
- Agree a timeframe for the above – generally it's recommended that it should be within 24 hours.
- Write down any consequences that will happen as a result of disclosing a slip or relapse. In other words, which partner boundaries have been crossed and what the consequence will be. For example, some partners insist on a period of separate bedrooms, further attendance at meetings, or going back into couple counselling. Partner boundaries should be established as part of their individual recovery.

Unfortunately, it's impossible to know exactly how you will feel and respond if, or more likely when, there is a slip, and even less chance of anticipating the fallout of a relapse. Ultimately you will have to make those decisions when, and if, it occurs, but having some kind of plan can help to protect your relationship from the fear of slips and relapses and strengthen personal resilience.

Evidence of recovery

I commonly hear partners asking 'How can I really know if he/ she's in recovery and not faking it? How do I know I'm not being manipulated and gaslighted again?' The honest answer is, 'you don't and you won't', or at least, not completely. There are no 100 per cent guarantees for anything in life and that includes your relationship. From the other perspective I hear addicted partners in recovery saying 'How can I prove that I'm not acting out? How can I prove I don't even want to act out anymore?' Again, you can't – you'll never be able to control how your partner thinks and feels, about you, or anything else.

Trust cannot be rebuilt by trying to prove that something 'hasn't' happened. In fact, it's impossible to prove that something 'hasn't' happened, which is why in a court of law, guilt has to be proved, not innocence. Unless there's proof that a crime has been committed, then the defendant is assumed innocent. But what you can do is see evidence that someone has changed in the way they think, feel and behave; that a life in recovery is being actively lived. Here are 10 measurable signs that couples can use to recognise that recovery is real.

1. The causes of the addiction have been identified and are being actively worked on. In other words, it's more than just managing the symptoms, it's digging out the root.
2. Recovery is 'active' – for example, attending meetings or going to therapy, keeping in touch with others in recovery for support and encouragement, perhaps maintaining a regular journal or reading recovery literature.
3. Life is healthier than before, such as taking regular exercise, eating a healthy diet, maintaining a positive life/work balance and managing stress through relaxation and hobbies.
4. Day-to-day relationships are better not just between the two of you, but also with children, extended family, friends and colleagues.
5. There's greater emotional connection and communication, including accepting and owning up to difficulties, mistakes and vulnerabilities.
6. There's a growing openness, compassion and empathy with others' emotional difficulties, mistakes and vulnerabilities.

7. Boundaries have improved and there's more assertiveness around managing personal needs, whether they are physical, emotional or sexual, and a greater ability to discuss those needs openly.
8. Life is approached proactively, rather than reactively. In other words, thinking ahead and taking positive action to prevent difficulties and problems arising or taking quick action to change things if they do.
9. There's a greater appreciation of the importance of living in the moment and staying in the present; attention is focused on enjoying what you have, rather than always wanting more.
10. Life's priority becomes living as someone with integrity who respects themselves and others and makes decisions in line with their values, rather than their emotions.

Ultimately, recovery from sex addiction is not about 'not' acting out, but about resolving the issues that led to the addiction in the first place. Addiction is a symptom of a mismanaged life. Seeing that life being managed healthily is the only true sign that someone is in recovery. And that is how couples can rebuild trust.

References

Arterburn, S., Martinkus, J.B. (2014) *Worthy of Her Trust – What you need to do to rebuild sexual integrity and win her back*. Colorado Springs, CO: Waterbrook Press.

Baucom, D.H., Snyder, D.K., Gordon, K.C. (2011) *Helping Couples Get Past the Affair – A clinician's guide*. New York: The Guildford Press.

Corley, D.M., Schneider, J.P. and Hook, J.N. (2012) Partner reactions to disclosure of relapse by self-identified sexual addicts. *Sexual Addiction and Compulsivity*, *19*(4): 265–283.

Gottman, J. (2012) *The Science of Trust*. New York: W.W. Norton.

Palmatier, J.J., Rovner, L. (2015) Credibility assessment: preliminary process theory, the polygraph process, and construct validity. *International Journal of Psychophysiology*, *95*: 3–13.

Tidwell Palmer, V. (2016) *Moving Beyond Betrayal, The 5-step boundary solution for partners of sex addicts*. Las Vegas: Central Recovery Press.

Weiss, R. (2017) *Out of the Doghouse – A step-by-step relationship-saving guide for men caught cheating*. Deerfield Beach, FL: Health Communications Inc.

Chapter 14

Developing and deepening intimacy

If trust is the hull of your new relation-ship, intimacy is the engine or the sails. Without intimacy, your relation-ship will go nowhere. Intimacy is often used as a euphemism for sex, but sex is only one aspect of intimacy, one that most often results from the others. All humans need intimacy, we need to feel known and loved for who we are, and we yearn to let others into our life so we can know and love them in return. True intimacy is a two-way experience, where both feel equally known and loved. No secrets, no defensiveness, but instead a relationship that is built on honesty and openness, where we are free to be ourselves, warts and all, and encouraged to grow to our full potential. Having said all that, intimacy does not come without anxiety. If we are going to let ourselves be fully known, we have to be vulnerable and courageous. We have to risk feeling rejected and getting it wrong, and at times, being disappointed and disappointing our partner. In *Erotic Intelligence*, Katehakis explains the dynamic dance of intimacy, warning that relationships are not fairy tales, but real-life, dynamic systems that force people to grow and change (Katehakis, 2010).

In this, our final chapter, we will explore what intimacy is and what it is not. We will look at different areas of intimacy and you'll find practical exercises to improve your intimate connection with each other. We will also focus on sexual intimacy, how sex and porn addiction can damage your most intimate intimacy and how you can reclaim and rebuild it. First we will look at why developing intimate relationships can be so difficult and some common blocks to intimacy, and why it's essential to overcome these if you want your relation-ship to set sail.

Blocks to intimacy

We begin to learn about intimacy from the day we are born and the level of intimacy you experienced in your childhood is going to have a direct impact on what you feel able to experience now. If you want to deepen your intimacy within the relationship, you need to be sure that any defences you've hitherto learnt, whether consciously or unconsciously, are being dismantled. One of the great joys of a truly intimate relationship is how it can fundamentally repair childhood wounds. Coupledom gives us the opportunity to rewrite our experiences of intimacy, and to pass on those positive experiences to the next generation.

There are three common blocks that can stop us enjoying the intimacy that we long for, each are basic survival patterns that may be playing underneath your conscious awareness. These blocks are trust, control and self-esteem (Collins & Collins, 2017) – we will look at each in a little more depth now.

- *Trust* – lack of trust impacts our ability to be vulnerable with another and take risks, as we saw in the last chapter. We fear intimacy because we think we'll be taken for granted or it will be turned and used against us. Furthermore, you might not trust yourself to get intimacy right.
- *Control* – learning that the only way to get your needs met is to be in control and to manipulate others emotionally. Rather than being truly vulnerable, you use intimacy as a way of getting your needs met, such as pretending to open up so your partner will open up to you, or being physically affectionate so you can get sex.
- *Low self-esteem* – struggling to cope if someone has a different reality to yourself, because it makes you doubt who you are and what you believe. Low self-esteem blocks intimacy because it impacts our ability to tolerate difference and hence we're less confident in sharing our truth or being able to hear another's, in case it's different.

If you're struggling with any of the above, then this is something you can consider working through in individual counselling; do also take a look at my other books and the previous chapter on trust. As you continue reading, particularly about the areas of intimacy, you might identify some areas that are harder for you than others – take this into counselling and talk to your partner about it. Talking about intimacy is an important first step to developing intimacy.

Below you can see a summary of what we've been talking about so far.

Intimacy is ...	Intimacy is not ...
Being your true self	Hiding yourself
Communicating openly	Expecting mind-reading
Being curious and learning about each other	Thinking you know everything about your partner or becoming a mind-reader
Acknowledging you and your partner as separate, autonomous individuals	Thinking and feeling the same
Respecting differences of perception	Seeing the world through the same eyes
Building resilience to sometimes feeling misunderstood, hurt and rejected	Always feeling comfortable and safe
Sometimes getting it wrong and disappointing your partner	Being perfect
Being willing to take responsibility for your thoughts, feelings and behaviours	Unconditional love

Before we end this section on blocks to intimacy, I want to share one other that often appears in the counselling room that can be linked to trust, control and low self-esteem, and that is 'not talking about it'. While I want to encourage you to focus on moving on in your relationship, the addiction is still there, and so is the impact on the partner. Some couples fear 'talking about it' lest it opens old wounds, or creates new ones, but avoiding talking about it means you're unable to be real with each other. How can any couple enjoy intimacy if there's a proverbial elephant in the room that one or both of you are trying to ignore? If you want to rebuild intimacy, you have to talk, however painful that might be, and in my experience when both couples are committed to getting closer, those conversations are never as bad as they fear. They are certainly not as bad as living with an elephant for the rest of your lives.

Areas of intimacy

There is no universally accepted inventory of intimacy types. Every book you read will offer you a slightly different list. In Chapter 6 we looked at the four key areas – emotional, intellectual, physical and recreational – you'll see these repeated below along with other areas that are often shared with me in the counselling room.

- *Emotional intimacy* – being similar in your emotional expression, whether that's getting angry or sad by the same things or being equally robust or sensitive.
- *Intellectual intimacy* – being on the same wavelength, sharing thoughts and ideas, being able to understand each other's thought processes.
- *Spiritual intimacy* – our relationship with our sense of spirituality, whether that's God, Gaia or just a general sense of something bigger than our individual humanity.
- *Physical intimacy* – physical affection, how it's shown and how often as well as being in tune with each other's physical demonstration of emotion.
- *Recreational intimacy* – being able to spend time together laughing, relaxing and having fun, whether that's as a couple, a family or with friends.
- *Professional intimacy* – the world of work, whether paid or unpaid, how important it is to us and how we engage in our respective professional roles.
- *Parenting intimacy* – how we bring up our children and our feelings about the role of parenting.
- *Aesthetic intimacy* – our sense of awe and wonder in the world, whether that's sharing a beautiful sunset, a work of art or, indeed, sharing the same lack of wonder.
- *Sexual intimacy* – we'll talk much more about this later in the chapter, but how we feel as sexual human beings and how we share that with each other.

As you can see, sexual intimacy is last in the list, but that doesn't mean it's of any less importance than the others. While sex undoubtedly delivers intimacy, it is also a consequence of other areas of intimacy and it should never be an end in itself. In *Worthy of Her Trust*, Arterburn and Martinkus warn readers against using other areas of intimacy just to pave the way for sex, stating: "Self-serving intimacy is not intimacy at all, it's manipulation" (Arterburn & Martinkus, 2014).

In Chapter 6 you had the opportunity to review the first four areas of intimacy within your relationship and consider the areas where you would like to grow as a couple. The same exercise can be repeated now with the list above. You will hopefully notice that there are some areas where your relationship is already strong – take time to celebrate those strengths. The exercises in the following section will help you to work on the areas where you'd like to develop or deepen intimacy.

Techniques for deepening intimacy

Intimacy cannot be improved simply through wishing it was better – it requires action. In order to strengthen intimacy it's important to identify specific behaviours in each area that will allow you to feel closer (Fife, 2016). Below are a number of techniques you can enjoy.

Intimacy requests

This is an exercise I regularly set couples within my practice to do between therapy sessions at home. While one of the outcomes of the exercise can be improved intimacy in any of the areas, the main objective is for each individual partner to become more aware of the behaviours that are most meaningful to them.

On alternate days, each partner makes an intimacy request of the other to be carried out during that day – or depending on what it is, the request might be made the night before. The request must be something that is easily achievable and must be non-sexual. For example, it might be share a cup of tea in bed with me in the morning, or join me taking the dog for a walk, or make the children's packed lunch for school, or watch a film or TV programme with me in the evening, or text me a compliment during the day. It really doesn't matter what it is, as long as it's achievable and means something to you. Your partner can of course refuse if they wish, but as it will be their turn to make a request tomorrow, that's unlikely. Try to think of a variety of different requests that pertain to the different areas of intimacy, but they don't have to be different every day if that's not achievable.

Although this exercise seems simple, it's often difficult to think about what your intimacy needs are, and remember that is the main objective: discovering what's important to you and learning to communicate it. The following exercise may help to give you more ideas.

Love needs

This exercise is adapted from the original version in my Dummies guide (Hall, 2010), and can help each of you to consider what is most important to you in order to feel loved. One of the mistakes that couples often make when trying to demonstrate their love for each other is following the commandment 'do unto others as you would have them do unto you'. While this is great guidance in many areas of life, it doesn't always work in intimate relationships because your needs may be very different from your partner's. What's more, our love needs change over the course of our life and in different circumstances. What follows is a list of common love needs – take a look through them individually and put them in your personal order of priority before sharing with each other.

- *Affection* – enjoying non-sexual physical touch, both receiving and giving.
- *Affirmation* – being complimented and positively praised verbally, or with gifts, for who you are and what you do.
- *Appreciation* – receiving thanks, whether through words or a gift, and being noticed for the contributions you make to the relationship and to the home and family.
- *Attention* – spending time together with the full attention of the other, whether that's sharing how your day has been or your inner thoughts and feelings.

- *Comfort* – being able to talk about difficult things and both giving and receiving physical tenderness and words of comfort.
- *Encouragement* – hearing positive words of encouragement when you're struggling with something, or being offered a helping hand.
- *Security* – receiving any words, gifts or actions that demonstrate commitment to the relationship.
- *Support* – hearing words of support or getting practical help.

How you show your love will depend on your personality and on the resources available, but remember to check out in concrete behavioural terms what is meaningful to you and your partner. In other words, rather than simply saying 'I want more appreciation', say 'I'd like you to thank me for cooking a meal'.

Five-a-day

This exercise is all about improving physical intimacy and it's another one I regularly set couples I work with for 'homework'. The objective is to make non-sexual affection a daily habit and beyond the obvious benefit of feeling nice, it also increases a couple's biochemical bonding.

We all know how important it is to get our five fruit and veg a day to have a healthy body, but until relatively recently, we weren't aware of how important regular physical touch is for healthy relationships. When we touch we release a chemical called oxytocin, the chemical that is responsible for bonding in intimate human relationships and the one that is critical between a newborn baby and its mother. Oxytocin is released when we touch and it inspires us to touch more. When couples literally lose touch with each other, their chemical bond weakens and they're more likely to drift apart. But the more you touch, the more oxytocin you produce and the more you want to touch and enjoy being touched. You get into a positive upward spiral and increase your emotional and biochemical bond.

The five-a-day exercise requires you as a couple to ensure you touch at least five times a day. That might be a kiss when you wake up, a kiss goodbye when you part and a kiss hello when you reunite. It might be holding hands when you walk, or an arm round the shoulder on the sofa, or a casual arm round the waist or touching hands when you speak. Any kind of non-sexual touch counts. Again, this may seem like an easy exercise, and indeed it is, but many couples, especially those who are recovering from sex or porn addiction, find they have got out of the habit of touching each other. The objective of five-a-day is to make a deliberate effort to touch until it becomes an automatic habit. And of course, you can have much more than five-a-day if you wish.

Caring behaviours exercise

This exercise is based on imago therapy and all about learning to touch the 'care button' (Luquet, 2007). The exercise works best when undertaken in a light, playful way and the objective is to help you each to identify what your partner already does that touches your care button, the things your partner used to do and the things you've always wanted them to do.

To complete the exercise, you'll need to write the following three headings and list your responses individually, and then share with each other. Your responses should be non-sexual ones – we'll come on to sexual intimacy shortly.

1. The things you do now that touch my care button and help me feel loved are …
2. The things you used to do that touched my care button and helped me feel loved were …
3. The things I've always wanted you to do that would touch my care button are …

When answering the final question, the goal is to think of the things that perhaps you've inhibited yourself from saying before because you thought it might sound too needy, or too selfish, or too silly, or extravagant. This is an opportunity to be completely honest about your intimacy needs. It's by no means a guarantee that they'll be met, but an opportunity to demonstrate your honesty, vulnerability and courage with each other. Let's move on now to exploring sexual intimacy.

Sexual intimacy

In the early stages of recovery, sex may have been the furthest thing from both of your minds. Or it may have been something that you avoided talking about at all costs, unable to know even how to begin the conversation. Depending on where you are in your recovery journey, sex may still be something neither of you, or only one of you, feels ready to consider, in which case, you should continue to work on other areas of intimacy first, and also look at the section later in this chapter on using a period of abstinence. However, for some individuals and couples, reclaiming their sex life is something that they're eager to do, as part of rebuilding trust and intimacy within the relationship.

Sex is an essential part of most couple relationships. When sex is good, not only do we feel good about ourselves as individuals, but we also feel good about our relationship. A good sex life can bond couples together and help them withstand the trials and tribulations of life. Sex means different things to different people at different stages of their life. And hence the role it plays in relationships will change, depending on how long you've been together and what life stage you're at.

The way that you each feel about sex and sexuality will depend on how your sex life was before the tidal wave of sex or porn addiction hit. If sex had always been a positive experience, then it will be easier to reclaim it, but if sex has been experienced negatively then it may a longer journey to rebuild sexual confidence and intimacy. If either individual within the couple has experienced sexual abuse in the past, whether as a child, adolescent or adult, then it can often be particularly difficult to find sexual confidence, especially if you haven't yet resolved those old trauma wounds.

Defining sexual intimacy

We learn about sex from a variety of sources. Initially it is within the family home and later from peers and partners. We also learn from our communities, our culture and from society, and increasingly we learn about sex through the media and online. There are often different sexual messages for men and for women, and whether you're straight or gay. Typically in western society men are brought up to believe that sex is a powerful drive that they must learn to manage through will, and emotions have little to do with it. Conversely, women may believe they are the bastions of sexual safety who must protect their bodies, hearts and souls from men's desires while denying any lust of their own. There are perhaps more mixed messages about sex today than there has ever been at any other time in history. While some strive for greater sexual liberation, others use statistics of sexual crime and abuse, and indeed sex addiction, as evidence that we should become more conservative. Defining sexual intimacy is challenging in a world that advocates freedom and diversity, but it is a task that each of us must embrace.

I would define sexual intimacy as any kind of sexual expression that is positive and fulfilling for both of you, emotionally, physically, psychologically and spiritually. I include 'spiritually' because for many people sex has a spiritual component, whether that's linked to a faith, or a way of articulating the profound feelings of connection and well-being that sex can evoke. In my previous books for partners and the addicted partner, positive sexuality is defined as being:

- in line with personal values
- respectful of self and others
- pleasurable
- mutually fulfilling (when partnered)
- not shameful
- confidence- and esteem-building.

There are few rights and wrongs in sex and each couple must decide for themselves what they are comfortable with and what will meet their personal needs. But if the core conditions above are met, then you're on the right track. Many couples in recovery find it helpful to put time aside to agree what they want from a sexual relationship and agree the vision that they're heading towards. One tool that many couples have found helpful is using the four-dimensional wheel of sexual experience (4-D Wheel), originally developed by Gina Ogden (Ogden, 2017). As you can see in Figure 14.1, there are four dimensions to sexual intimacy – spiritual, mental, physical and emotional. When you are able to experience each of these four

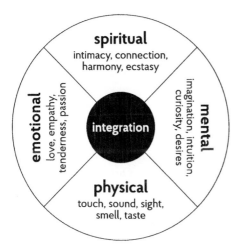

spiritual
intimacy, connection,
harmony, ecstasy

emotional
love, empathy,
tenderness, passion

integration

mental
imagination, intuition,
curiosity, desires

physical
touch, sound, sight,
smell, taste

Figure 14.1 4-D wheel

dimensions, you have a sexual experience that is fully integrated. In other words, you share an experience where heart, body, mind and soul are all in harmony. This wheel can be used alone, or with a therapist, to expand your awareness and promote growth.

It may take time to build a sexual relationship where you both feel fulfilled and comfortable, and there may be hiccups along the way, some of which may be painful. But knowing you're working together with a common goal can provide the necessary motivation and momentum required. If this feels like a difficult conversation to have alone, a couple counsellor or sex therapist can help.

What about masturbation?

Whether you choose to masturbate as individuals within your relationship is a matter of basic human rights and, some would say, self-care (Katehakis, 2010). Some couples are comfortable with the fact that their partner masturbates and consider this a personal matter; others believe it's information that should be shared. Some partners understandably worry that if the addicted partner is masturbating, they are continuing to act out and may be withholding from the relationship, while others see mindful masturbation (i.e. without any visual imagery or fantasy) as an essential part of relapse prevention. If you struggle to come to an agreement on this topic, then do discuss with others you trust in recovery or discuss in couple counselling. What's essential is that you are honest, even if you have to agree to disagree.

Managing sexual intimacy fears

Being sexual is part of the nature of being human. We are all sexual beings, whether we're sexually active or not. Our sexuality includes our gender, our thoughts and our feelings about sex, whether they are positive or negative. It includes our sexual orientation, our desires and our sexual behaviours. Feeling comfortable and confident about our sexuality is essential for positive self-esteem, but regrettably, many partners feel as if their sexual identity has been contaminated by their partner's sexual addiction, and addicted partners may fear their sexuality is innately damaged, dangerous and out of control.

It's normal to worry about sex when you're a couple recovering from sex or porn addiction, as it would be getting into a car again after a car crash, whether the accident was your responsibility or not. There will be some fears that are common to both of you and some that are unique to you as individuals. The first step in overcoming them is to be honest with yourselves, and with each other, about those fears, so you can work together to overcome them. Below are the most common fears.

- *Feeling inadequate* – both partners can lose their sexual confidence because of addiction, and if your sexual self-confidence was low in the first place, addiction undoubtedly makes it worse. Partners in particular can worry about living up to porn stars or people the addicted partner acted out with, and the addicted partner may feel inadequate to prove that's not the case.
- *Feeling distracted* – ensuring you stay in the present moment is key to avoiding distraction, but nonetheless, it's common for both partners and addicted partners to be distracted by intrusive thoughts and images of past acting out behaviours. Some may come from memory and some from imagination; either way, they

are damaging and get in the way of being able to enjoy sexual intimacy.

- *Fearing your partner is distracted* – this is equally as damaging as being distracted because while you're worrying about what your partner is thinking and feeling, you're not being fully present yourself. Couples have to work together to develop verbal and non-verbal ways of letting their partner know that they are fully present in the moment, not reliving or imagining anything from the past.

- *Fearing sex will hinder addiction recovery* – potentially this is a distraction during a sexual experience, but it can also block couples from initiating one or enjoying the aftermath. Partners often worry that having sex will ignite the addicted partner's libido and they will be more likely to act out. Conversely, some worry that 'not' having sex could also trigger acting out and hence initiate sex when they don't really want to. For some addicted partners having sex, or not having sex, can indeed increase cravings, and as well as developing strategies to manage this, they also need to reassure their partner that they are using those strategies.

Sex can, and does get better, but it takes time and a committed motivation to want it for yourself, as well as for the relationship. Regrettably, sexual dysfunctions are also common, which we will explore now.

Resolving sexual dysfunctions

Sexual problems can affect us all at different times of our life and at different stages of the relationship, but they are particularly common in couples recovering from sex addiction. This can be particularly frustrating for both of you and can create further feelings of insecurity. Some partners perceive their mate's lack of arousal or difficulty experiencing orgasm as a personal indictment of their lack of attractiveness or of their addicted partner's lack of desire to be sexual. For the addicted partner it can generate similar fears, along with a fear that if they're unable to perform, their partner will take it personally. But genital functioning does not give a fair representation of what's going on inside anyone's head or heart. In this section we will look at the most common problems that can affect men and women and some advice for overcoming them. If problems persist, or if they have been long-standing and not connected to the addiction, then do seek help from an accredited sex therapist.

Erection problems

Erection problems are a common side effect of heavy pornography use and it is often referred to as PIED (porn-induced erectile dysfunction). This is because constant novel sexual stimuli can increase the arousal threshold, thus making it harder to be aroused with physical contact alone. While common, the good news is that it normally resolves itself once porn has ceased for a period of time. The most common psychological cause is anxiety, and as the addicted partner, you may feel under even more pressure than usual to ensure that sex is enjoyable for both of you and demonstrate your desire for your partner. The problem with anxiety is that it tends to create a self-fulfilling prophecy: the more anxious you are that you won't get an erection, the more chance there is that you won't, and hence the more anxious you become. The best way to cure erection problems is to understand that it's not personal and give yourselves time. An understanding and supportive partner can help to reduce the anxiety and the more you can stop worrying about getting an erection, the more likely it will occur.

Female arousal difficulties

In most respects, female arousal difficulties are the same as male problems with erection, but they're less obvious and less likely to stop you having sex. But continuing with sex if a woman's not physically aroused can be painful and certainly gets in the way of being able to enjoy orgasm. A supportive and understanding partner is again essential as well as learning to relax and take time to find the best ways of being sensual and sexually stimulated.

Premature ejaculation

Most men will ejaculate faster in times of stress or after a long period without ejaculation – both of which are common when recovering as a couple from sex addiction. It can also be a common response to feelings of guilt and shame. Like erection problems, anxiety is known to contribute to quick ejaculation and therefore reducing anxiety is essential. When partners can be patient and supportive the problem should resolve itself on its own. If the problem has been long-standing then there are additional techniques that can help, such as ensuring you focus fully on physical sensations and doing pelvic floor exercises.

Difficulty reaching orgasm (his and hers)

Struggling to experience orgasm is a common problem for both men and women recovering from sex and porn addiction, whether you're the person with the addiction or the partner. The most common reason is stress and anxiety, but it can also be a consequence of heavy porn use. As with all sexual problems, your first line of attack is stress management and relaxation, in addition to a supportive and understanding partner. You may also find that changing stimulation techniques and pelvic floor exercises will also help.

Mismatched sexual desire

Many couples struggle with mismatched sexual desire and this may have been a problem long before the addiction was recognised. Each couple has to work out between themselves how much sex is OK in their relationship and there's no 'right' amount of sex that you should have. If you want sex every day and your partner wants it once a month, you're both perfectly normal, but you'll need to work together to find a compromise that both of you feel happy with. Negotiating different sexual needs can be tricky because emotions often run high. Often one partner feels the other is withholding and rejecting, while the other feels their partner's demands are unreasonable. During recovery there can also be fears that if the person with the higher sex drive is the addicted partner, they will relapse if their needs aren't met. But conversely, if the partner with the lower sex drive is the one with the addiction, there may be fears that they must already be acting out elsewhere.

The first step to resolving the dispute is to accept that your differences do not necessarily relate to the addiction at all and that neither of you are in the wrong. When both of you can accept each other as different, rather than wrong, you can cooperate with each other to find a solution. Both partners need to take equal responsibility for creating a relaxed and sensual environment within the home where sex is more likely to occur. To avoid any miscommunication, some couples agree 'sex-free days' where they can feel free to get close with no expectations. As discussed earlier, focusing on affection and sensuality can significantly increase the likelihood that sex will occur, as well as ensuring basic conditions are being met.

We will move on now to explore some techniques that can help you to develop and deepen your sexual connection.

Understanding sex therapy

If you're struggling with developing or deepening sexual intimacy in any way, whether that's due to an emotional, psychological or physical problem, then do consider working with an accredited sex therapist that is also trained in working with couples and sex addiction. Sex therapy will provide each of you with a safe place to talk about your sexual concerns and your therapist will also provide you with homework assignments to help you understand any unconscious causes and overcome them. The most common treatment intervention used is sensate focus, which is a highly individualised behavioural therapy technique that has been rigorously evaluated (Weeks & Gambescia, 2009). Sensate focus serves many functions, including helping partners become more aware of physical sensations, learning to communicate sensual and sexual needs and desires, learning to enjoy touch that is non-sexual, creating a positive relational experience, enhancing the level of love, care, commitment, cooperation and sexual desire and resolving sexual dysfunctions. If medical intervention is required, an accredited sex therapist will also be able to advise you on an appropriate referral. You can find more details about sex therapy at www.corsrt.org.uk.

Techniques for developing and deepening sexual intimacy

Before we start exploring this topic, let me reiterate that sexual intimacy results from developing and deepening other areas of intimacy first. There are two key reasons for this. Firstly, if you're not able to be comfortable with other forms of intimacy then one, or both of you, may become too dependent on a successful sexual relationship in order to feel close. Not only is this unrealistic, because sexual relationships inevitably wax and wane, but it also puts undue pressure on both of you to make sex fantastic every time, which again, inevitably is unrealistic. Secondly, if you're unable to find the courage to be vulnerable within other areas of your relationship, it's highly unlikely you'll be able to fully experience sexual intimacy. You may enjoy having sex with your partner, but it will not be true intimacy. As we saw in the 4-D Wheel, sexual intimacy means integrating body, mind, heart and soul, and that requires a greater degree of courage, vulnerability and trust than any other area of intimacy. So my strong advice is to master these skills in other areas of intimacy before reading on.

Using a period of abstinence

This may seem like an odd way to start writing about developing sexual intimacy, but if you want to check that you're not over-dependent on sex to feel close as a couple, it's a great place to start. Some addiction professionals insist on a period of abstinence, as part of the addicted partner's recovery, including masturbation as well as partnered sex. There are many reasons for this, and while some people really struggle, others welcome it as an opportunity to reset their sexual appetite and focus on recovery. Some partners also welcome the restriction, while others feel this is overly censorial and intrusive on their intimate couple life, not to mention feeling hugely unfair if they have always enjoyed sex. You may have already worked through your period of abstinence together, but if you haven't it may be something you wish to consider, as there are advantages for you both. Abstinence allows time to:

- Focus on rebuilding sexual self-confidence, physically and emotionally

- Strengthen your individual recovery journeys
- Work on rewriting unwanted and intrusive negative thoughts and images
- Continue rebuilding trust
- Focus on developing other ways of being intimate and close
- Create confidence that your relationship can survive without sex
- Develop confidence that you're appreciated and needed in non-sexual ways
- Focus on your conditions for good sex (see next section)

Some couples who have already been through a period of abstinence but discover they are still struggling to connect sexually agree to a further period of semi-abstinence, for example agreeing no genital contact, but focusing on building physical intimacy and sensuality. This is a strategy often very effectively used in sex therapy to help couples learn more about their sexual selves and each other and kick-start their sexual relationship (see the box Understanding sex therapy for more details).

Create the right conditions

Every time you have sex, whether that's after a period of abstinence or not, it's important to know that you're ready. Ready emotionally, relationally and physically. Having sex is going to feel risky at first, and to minimise those risks it makes sense to ensure your core conditions are right. Your core conditions are likely to include:

- *Your emotional needs* – for sex to be a positive experience, you each need to be in the right frame of mind. That means choosing a time when you're not preoccupied with work or other responsibilities and when you're feeling in a good enough emotional space. It may not be realistic to wait until you're both completely free of any anxiety or challenging emotions, but they should feel manageable.
- *Your relationship needs* – if there is a lot of tension in your relationship then right now may not be the time to have sex. If there are problems that can be resolved, then deal with them first; if not, then ensure you're confident that the two of you are equally

committed to working on them. Each of you also needs to be confident that your physical appearance and/or sexual performance won't be judged.

• *Your physical needs* – in addition to trusting you can each be open about what you need physically to become aroused and stimulated, you also need to know your physical environment is sufficiently relaxed. For example, that the lighting and temperature are right and that you won't be disturbed or overheard. In addition, most people need to feel reasonably awake, and sober, in order to enjoy sex. They also need to feel in good health and not in too much pain or discomfort.

Building sensuality

Once you've determined your conditions for sex have been met for you both, you need to get started. Being sexual is one end of a continuum with being affectionate at the other end and sensuality somewhere in between. Assuming you've already worked on your physical intimacy and you are getting your five-a-day, it will be much easier to turn a touch into a caress, a hug into a hold and a kiss into a smooch. Touching in more intimate places and allowing increasing skin on skin contact. If you have plenty of free together time, then building sensuality may be sufficient for naturally slipping into more sexual encounters, but if you lead busy lives, or have children, or both, then you may need to be more strategic.

A colleague of mine often jokes that the best sex aid a busy couple can have is a diary. Waiting for sex to happen spontaneously, when the mood is right, may be a rarity, and hence agreeing time when you can consciously create the mood, may be more pragmatic and successful. There is a common myth that sex should always be spontaneous, but planning ahead can help to build erotic anticipation as well as allowing time for any fears and anxieties to be talked through.

In my work with couples I often talk about learning to 'go on amber'. Using a traffic light as a metaphor, when you're on red you definitely don't want sex and therefore don't want to do anything sexual. When you're on green, you definitely do want sex and probably won't have any problem enjoying it. But the vast majority of the time you're on amber. In other words, the answer's not yes or no, it's maybe. Going on amber means agreeing that both of you are hoping the lights will go green, but if the lights go red, you stop.

It's much easier to feel comfortable building sensuality if you know you can stop if you want to. Some couples make the mistake of only initiating sex when they're 100 per cent confident that both of them are equally enthusiastic, but in the early stages of recovery, this may rarely be the case. If either of you knows that you don't want sex, then it's important to feel confident in saying no. Knowing that, while your partner may be disappointed, they will be understanding and gracious about it. Furthermore, if you do begin to build sensuality, but one of you changes your mind, it's equally important to know the decision will be understood and accepted. Having the conversation beforehand about what you will do if you decide to stop can help to avoid awkwardness, guilt and resentments.

Trying new things

Many people recovering from sex addiction, both partners and addicted partners, can be fearful of being sexually adventurous and trying new things. But for some, doing something completely new can be an effective way of reclaiming their sex lives. Obviously you both need to be ready to take this step, and many couples never feel the need to, or have the desire to, but if you do then make sure it's something you investigate together. One couple I worked with chose to explore the world of tantric sex and found a new depth of connection, intimacy and erotica that neither had ever experienced before and it revolutionised their sex life. There's much more advice on developing your sex life in the book *Erotic Intelligence* (Katehakis, 2010).

There are many hurdles for couples recovering their individual sexuality and sex lives from sex addiction, and deepening their sexual intimacy. However, as long as you both remain committed to your individual recovery and continue to deepen other areas of intimacy, then sexual fulfilment can be found again. Indeed, it can be better than ever. I will let our couples have the last word in this chapter.

> The saddest thing is that it took recovery to increase our levels of intimacy; the good thing is that recovery enabled us to become healthy and more intimate with each other. (Addicted partner)

We are both more open and intimate with each other, more likely to share feelings and emotions. More likely to agree to time out if we are getting argumentative and more able to de-escalate an emotionally charged situation; also more likely to say sorry and try to make peace with each other. (Addicted partner)

We are definitively closer now and my husband is a lot more open with me. I think it is generally a happier home for us and the children and we all make more time for each other. (Partner)

I've never experienced a relationship as good as this and it tracks back to the work I've done on myself as well as the work we've both put into our relationship. We share our inner worlds, we laugh much more, we apologise when we're wrong ... all glimpses I saw before, now these changes feel enduring and deep. (Partner)

We are now closer than ever before. (Addicted partner)

References

Arterburn, S., Martinkus, J.B. (2014) *Worthy of Her Trust – What you need to do to rebuild sexual integrity and win her back* (p. 86). Colorado Springs, CO: Waterbrook Press.

Collins, P.C., Collins, G.N. (2017) *A Couples Guide to Sexual Addiction, A step-by-step plan to rebuild trust and restore intimacy*. Avon, MA: Adams Media.

Fife, S.T. (2016) *Aspects of Intimacy, Techniques for the couple therapist, essential interventions from the experts* (edited by G. Weeks, S.T. Fife, C.M. Peterson), pp. 146–150. New York: Routledge.

Hall, P. (2010) *Improving Your Relationship for Dummies*. Chichester: John Wiley & Sons.

Hall, P.A. (2016) *Sex Addiction – The partner's perspective*. London: Routledge.

Katehakis, A. (2010) *Erotic Intelligence, Igniting hot, healthy sex while in recovery from sex addiction*. Deerfield Beach, FL: Health Communications Inc.

Luquet, W. (2007). *Short Term Couples Therapy – The imago model in action*. New York: Routledge.

Ogden, G. (2017) *Exploring Desire & Intimacy, A workbook for creative clinicians*. New York: Routledge.

Weeks, G., Gambescia, N. (2009) A systemic approach to sensate focus. In *Systemic Sex Therapy* (edited by K. Hertlein, G. Weeks, N. Gambescia), pp. 341–362. New York: Routledge.

Summary for couple therapists – moving on together

If the couple has agreed that they wish to rebuild their relation-ship, then the focus will be on rebuilding trust and developing and deepening intimacy. Before this can happen, it's essential that each partner is aware that they are rebuilding their relationship as individ-uals who are both in recovery from the impact of the addiction. While acting out behaviours will hopefully be in the past, the consequences will continue, and each must accept responsibility for building both personal and couple resilience. The key tasks for the therapist are helping each partner understand the process of recovering from addiction and trauma and developing strategies for letting go of the past and focusing on the future that each of them desires. Therapy will focus on:

- Psychoeducating on recovery from trauma and being in recovery from addiction
- Helping couples to communicate their ongoing recovery needs and accept their partner's with compassion
- Encouraging couples to take responsibility for self-care and to continue to get support from others outside of their relationship
- Overcoming any residual shame and blame that may hinder their progress
- Writing a partnership contract that commits to their individual recovery and supports their partner's recovery
- Understanding and facilitating the journey of self-forgiveness and forgiveness of each other

- Helping the person with the addiction to become trustworthy in a way that is meaningful to their partner
- Discussing with the couple how to differentiate between a slip and a relapse and what strategies they'll employ if either occur
- Facilitating the couple in developing their relationship in every aspect of intimacy

While helping couples to move on together, therapists should continue to be mindful of the individual recovery journeys, in particular how each partner is coping with triggers and the other partner's capacity to demonstrate empathy when they occur. Before ending therapy, clients should be made aware that it's normal to experience triggers from trauma, and addiction, for many years after acting out has ceased, and this should not be seen as a sign of weakness or failure. Before ending therapy, clients can develop a future plan for how to manage these triggers and continue to focus on building trust and intimacy.

Conclusion

As I reach the end of the 'hardest book I've ever written', I find the conclusion is no easier to write. I hope this book has helped each of you, both the partner and the addicted partner, to gain more insight and understanding of what's happened to you, to each other, and to your relationship. I also hope that you have developed more resources to survive the tidal wave of sex and porn addiction and consider if your relation-ship can survive. And, whatever your decision for the future, I hope you feel stronger and better equipped for the journey ahead.

Couples can, and do, not only survive sex addiction, but also thrive and grow as a result of it. Some do this together, but for some the wiser decision is to continue their life journey apart. Neither is an easy choice, nor guarantees a smooth journey. Both require the compassion and commitment to let go of the painful past and learn to trust yourself, and others, again. Both require the courage to navigate uncharted waters and to dare to dream of bright new horizons.

Remember, whichever direction you go, you are not alone. Many others have travelled before you, and many are continuing to travel by your side. Some are sailing solo, others are two-person crafts, but all can look forward to a future of happiness and wholeness.

Perhaps the only way to end this book is to say, 'Anchors away and bon voyage'!

Further reading and resources

Books about sex and porn addiction

CBT for Compulsive Sexual Behaviour, A Guide for Professionals, Thaddeus Birchard (Routledge)

Confronting Porn, A guide for Christians, Paula Hall (Naked Truth Resources)

Facing Love Addiction: Giving yourself the power to change the way you love, Pia Mellody (Harper One)

International Handbook of Sexual Addiction, edited by Thaddeus Birchard (Routledge)

Making Advances: A comprehensive guide for treating female sex and love addicts, Marnie Ferree (SASH)

Out of the Shadows – Understanding sex addiction, Patrick Carnes (Hazelden).

Overcoming Sex Addiction, A self-help guide, Thaddeus Birchard (Routledge)

Sex Addiction 101 – A basic guide to healing from sex, porn, and love addiction, Robert Weiss (Health Communications Inc.)

Sex Addiction 101 – The workbook, Robert Weiss (Health Communications Inc.)

The Porn Trap – The essential guide to overcoming problems caused by pornography, Wendy Maltz & Larry Maltz (Harper)

Your Brain on Porn, Internet pornography and the emerging science of addiction, Gary Wilson (Commonwealth Publishing)

Understanding and Treating Sex and Pornography Addiction (2nd edition), Paula Hall (Routledge)

Books for partners

Mending a Shattered Heart – A guide for partners of sex addicts, edited by Stefanie Carnes (Gentle Path Press)

Moving Beyond Betrayal, The 5-step boundary solution for partners of sex addicts, Vicki Tidwell Palmer (CRP)

Sex Addiction – A guide for partners, Paula Hall (Routledge)
Surviving Disclosure, A partner's guide for healing the betrayal of intimate trust, Jennifer Schneider & Deborah Corley (Recovery Resources Press)
Your Sexually Addicted Spouse, Barbara Steffens & Martha Means (New Horizon Press)

Books about relationships and general self-help

A Couples Guide to Sexual Addiction, A step-by-step plan to rebuild trust and restore intimacy, Paldrom Collins & George Collins (Adams Media)
Cognitive Behavioural Couple Therapy, Michael Worrell (Routledge)
Daring Greatly. How the courage to be vulnerable transforms the way we live, love, parent and lead, Brene Brown (Penguin)
Erotic Intelligence, Igniting Hot, Healthy Sex While in Recovery from Sex Addiction, Alexandra Katehakis (HCI)
Getting Past the Affair, A program to help you cope, heal and move on – together or apart, Douglas Snyder, Donald Baucom & Kristina Gordon (Guilford)
Help Your Children Cope with Your Divorce, Paula Hall (Vermillion)
Helping Couples Get Past the Affair, A clinician's guide, Donald Baucom, Douglas Snyder & Kristina Gordon (Guilford)
How Can I Forgive You, The courage to forgive, the freedom not to, Janis Abrams Spring (Harper)
How to Have a Healthy Divorce, Paula Hall (Vermillion)
Improving Your Relationship – for Dummies, Paula Hall (Wiley)
Out of the Doghouse – A step-by-step relationship-saving guide for men caught cheating, Robert Weiss (HCI)
Relationships in Recovery – A guide for sex addicts who are starting over, Linda Hatch (Pentacle)
Techniques for the Couple Therapist, essential interventions from the experts, edited by Gerald Weeks, Stephen Fife & Colleen Peterson (Routledge)
The Couples Therapy Companion, A cognitive behaviour workbook, Russell Grieger (Routledge)
Worthy of Her Trust, What you need to do to rebuild sexual integrity and win her back, Stephen Arterburn & Jason Martinkus (Water Brook)

Additional resources

APSATS (The Association of Partners of Sex Addicts Trauma Specialists). Therapy and training on betrayal trauma, based in the USA. www.apsats. org
ATSAC (Association for the Treatment of Sexual Addiction and Compulsivity). The UK's professional association for sex addiction professionals, www.atsac.co.uk

ISAT (Institute for Sex Addiction Training). Accredited diploma training and CPD for professionals in Sex and Porn Addiction, www.thelaurelcentre. co.uk/sex-addiction-training

Kick Start Recovery Programme – a free online resource created by Paula Hall to help individuals struggling with sex and porn addiction, www. sexaddictionhelp.co.uk

The Laurel Centre – International services for Addiction Recovery and Support for Partners developed by Paula Hall, www.thelaurelcentre.co.uk

The Naked Truth Project – a national charity providing resources and services for porn recovery and education for parents and pastoral carers, www.thenakedtruthproject.com

Recovery Nation – a free online resource for addicts, partners and couples, www.recoverynation.com

SAA (Sex Addicts Anonymous), www.saa-recovery.org.uk

SLAA (Sex and Love Addicts Anonymous), www.slaauk.org

StopSo, Specialist Treatment Organisation for the Prevention of Sex Offending, contact info@stopso.org.uk

Your Brain on Porn – a science-based website that provides information about the impact of pornography and recovery advice for those whose porn use is a problem, www.yourbrainonporn.com

Index

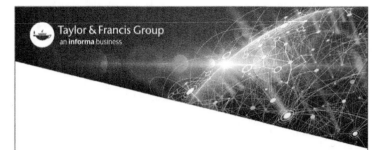